RETENTION!

How to plug
THE #1 PROFIT LEAK
in your dental practice

DR JESSEGREEN

RETENTION!

How to Plug the #1 Profit Leak in your Dental Practice

Visit Jesse's website: **www.drjessegreen.com**

National Library of Australia Cataloging-in-Publication entry

Author: Dr Jesse Green
Title: Retention! How to Plug the #1 Profit Leak in your Dental Practice
ISBN: 978-0-9923058-0-2
Subjects: Practice Management, Marketing (Dental practice)

Dewey number: 658.804

Author photo by Raul Ortiz de Lejarazu Machin
Cover design by Meen Thamsongsana
Layout and internal design by Setthawut Pattanasuwimol

Some dentists live in denial. They believe that if they do what they have been trained to do, then success should follow. They don't know what to do when this doesn't happen. Jesse asks our profession to look at themselves, to face their fears, to change and lead and ultimately by hard work to really enjoy their secret desires of success. Don't read this book and let it slide. Your answers are here. Just implement them!

Dr. Mark Miller, Dental As Anything

Jesse so eloquently highlights the behavioural science behind what patients may think – a missing part of the puzzle as to why good dental clinicians may not have the clinic that they have always desired! A must-read book for any clinician who desires insight to the other side of the dental chair.

Dr. Dail Kim, Riverside Dental

If you want increased profitability, a loyal team that performs at the highest standards and a very long queue of your ideal patients waiting to see you… then "Retention!" will show you how to achieve that and more.

"Retention!" artfully blends cutting edge 'modern day' marketing strategies with the timeless principles of business growth. It is an easy read and offers no-nonsense strategies for how to grow a successful dental practice. I particularly liked the tools, templates and checklists in the companion Implementation Workbook. These saved me the hassle and heartache of having to invent them myself. It is sure to become the 'Bible' for every dental practice owner.

What makes this book so refreshing is that rather than being based on academic theory, it draws from Jesse's experience operating practices in both the pre and post-GFC economies. It shows you how to not only survive, but thrive, in any economic climate.

This is essential reading for any dentist who wants to have a practice that is stress free, fun and gives them the financial rewards they desire.

Dr. David Dugan, Dentist

This book is recommended reading whether you are starting your practice or have an established practice. It is easy reading with real-life stories from Jesse's practicing career. By implementing the book's strategies we're quickly moving towards our ideal practice and lifestyle.

Dr. Barry Young, Riverside Dental

CONTENTS

FOREWORD

All too often businesses, of all kinds, focus the majority of their attention, energy and resources on acquiring new customers, with little to no thought on retaining the ones they already have. Over 30 years of working with many businesses, across virtually every industry, I have found this to be a consistent issue and one that needs some serious attention.

That's why Dr Jesse Green's book 'RETENTION!' really resonated with me. A book focused entirely on helping dental practices to strategically retain their most valuable asset, their existing patients.

Having had the pleasure of working with Jesse in his environment, specifically coaching dentists to build their practices and make them more resilient, it soon became very obvious that he was not only a very smart man, but also someone who really has walked the walk.

Jesse shares his knowledge and his own personal experience as a very successful dental practitioner, but he does it in a genuine and compassionate way. He understands the challenges that every dental clinic faces and provides strategic, structured and easy to implement advice.

What I like the most about Jesse's take on retention is that he goes to great lengths to show why it is such an essential and important element of a successful dental practice. He introduces the concept of becoming a trusted advisor to patients, as opposed to a transactional deliverer of a service. This is a major point of differentiation that every successful dental practice understands.

As I read through 'RETENTION!' I saw page after page of valuable information and advice, shared in a simple, no nonsense manner, with Jesse's passion for the topic shining through.

This is a book that smart dentists will keep close, reading it regularly, taking action on the advice Jesse offers and making their practice increasingly resilient, profitable and successful in every way.

Andrew Griffiths
Australia's #1 Small Business Author, 12 Books now sold in over 60 countries.

INTRODUCTION

A smile is a curve that sets everything straight.
Phyllis Diller

To be a dentist is to belong to a noble profession. We work within one of the most intimate parts of the human body to restore the physical health as well as the emotional well-being of our patients.

Caring for our patients is a responsibility we all take seriously. We constantly look for better ways to improve the lives of patients and in the past twenty years or so there have been many clinical advances that have allowed us to do this.

However, during the same period, the environment in which we operate has changed just as dramatically and remains in a state of flux. Everything is changing. That much is obvious. However, what is less obvious is the impact that these changes have had on the well-being of dentists and their families.

As I travel around the country talking to dentists in all sorts of practices, ranging from traditional family practices to high-end cosmetically driven practices, from metropolitan to regional practices, many dentists tell me they're feeling anxious about what the future holds. I have come across numerous dentists who have defaulted on loans, some who have lost their homes and many who are making less income as well as seeing the value of their practices diminish. Many dentists are feeling anxious about the shifting sands of the environment in which we practice.

I decided to write this book to help alleviate that anxiety.

The book is based on the premise that practice viability is correlated to the strength of the patient base. Indeed, other than the dentists themselves, the patient base is regarded as the number one asset of the practice because it represents stability and predictability of earnings. The corollary is, of course, that the loss of patients represents the number one profit leak within a dental practice.

This book is designed to show you how to plug the profit leak in your dental practice in the face of increased competition. Mastering the principles within this book will free you from anxiety and set you on a path of prosperity.

The strategies in this book are not business theories or based on hypothetical situations. Instead, they have been sharpened on the whetstone of the market and are the same strategies I have used to grow my own practices and those of my clients.

I believe that the community and the profession itself are best served by ensuring the viability of independently owned private practices. We have seen what happens in other industries when corporatisation and the development of virtual monopolies or duopolies goes unchecked.

The good news is that despite all the market turmoil, there has never been a better time to build a remarkable practice. You just need to know how.

This book will help you come to understand what the changing times mean for you and your family. You will also learn why the first step of any marketing campaign must be patient retention. I will outline the factors that contribute to patient retention through loyalty and how it can be cultivated with specific intent.

This book will also show you how to minimise cancellations and "fail to attends" which are often the precursors to patient loss, not to mention the negative impact they have on productivity.

I will then discuss effective ways to harness the power of patient loyalty as a means to drive practice growth. If you master these, you will never need to "market" again.

A word of caution: at first glance, some of these strategies may seem deceptively simple, so simple, in fact, that you might not implement them. But simple is not the same as easy.

The practice you have now is based on thoughts and actions of the past. If you want a different future, you will need to adapt to the new reality and do things differently. Nothing will change without implementation. To know and not do, is not to know.

Some might read this book and think, "I already do that" or "I've tried that". And if you have all the patient flow you can handle, then I salute you. However, if you're like most dentists who have "tried that" and find patient flow is still below par, then I am going to challenge you to really scrutinise what you do and see if you can do it better. In the words of John W Gardner, *"Excellence is doing ordinary things extraordinarily well."*

As you read through this book, take the time to highlight pertinent sections, make notes and, most importantly, take action. It is my hope that this book will be dog-eared and battered by the time I see you.

A Note to Specialists

While operating a specialist practice has some obvious similarities to general practice, it has some clear differences as well.

Dental specialists are often in the position of serving two different clients – the patient and the referring dentist. Some specialists find that the lifetime value of a patient is confined to a single episode of care whereas other specialists treat patients for many years.

Some specialists market directly to the public, while others operate a referral-based practice. Most specialists operate a practice that is a combination of the two. Irrespective of the type of specialist practice, referring general practitioners represent a source of patient flow that is pre-qualified and virtually free of acquisition price.

The principles of patient retention are well documented throughout the general section of this book. However, where necessary, I have included "A Note to Specialists", which contains advice on how to apply the information in that particular chapter to retain and grow your network of referring general practitioners.

As the profession continues to face increased competition and an operating environment that continually changes, most specialist practices will find they need to develop strategies to retain both patients and their referral network. While the different strategies will be based on the same principles, it is important for specialists to develop and implement separate plans for each group.

Getting the Most Out of this Book

Very simply, the aim of this book is to help dentists and specialists take practical steps to retain their client base whether that be patients or referring practitioners.

This book provides you with both the relevant background information as well as a series of action steps to help you implement all you have learned.

The power of an idea is only ever in its implementation. To assist you to implement the material in the book, I have created a companion workbook, which contains checklists, cheat sheets and other resources.

You can download it from:
www.drjessegreen.com/retention/workbook

1

THE CHANGING FACE OF DENTISTRY

Do not pray for easy lives.
Pray to be stronger men.

—

John F Kennedy

THE CHANGING FACE OF DENTISTRY

Not so long ago, making a good living as a dentist was easy. These were the halcyon days – before the Global Financial Crisis (GFC) hit – a time when people were feeling optimistic about the future. There was a seemingly never-ending supply of patients willing to spend money on their dental health and an undersupply of dentists on hand to look after them. Demand far outstripped supply.

However, in recent years the dental profession has been caught in a perfect storm. Making a living as a dentist is harder than it has ever been and is set to get harder still. As a profession, we are entering uncharted waters.

Challenges Facing the Profession

Although the profession is facing challenges on many fronts, there are four major challenges that pose a significant threat to the viability of independently owned private practices.

1. Oversupply of Dentists and Auxiliaries

In Australia, access to and affordability of dental care has become increasingly prominent on the national political agenda. Successive Federal Governments have sought to address the undersupply of dentists by dramatically increasing the number of locally trained dentists.

According to the Health Workforce by Numbers report, the number of dental students who completed courses leading to provisional registration increased from 220 in 2004 to 478 in 2012. However, what this statistic does not account for is the cohort that is set to graduate from newer dental courses. The report indicates that in 2012, 616 domestic and international students commenced courses that will lead to provisional registration as dental practitioners (currently defined as a dentist).[1] These students are expected to enter the profession in 2016 and according to some commentators, may graduate to unemployment.[2]

In addition to the locally trained dentists, permanent visas were granted to 209 dentists in 2011-12, while another 163 temporary, sub-class 457 visas were granted to overseas dentists.

Not only have the numbers of dentists increased, so too have the number of dental auxiliaries such as dental hygienists, dental therapists and oral health therapists. In the period from 2006 to 2011, total registrations for these three groups increased, from 2531 to 3479, representing an increase of 37% over this period.[1]

Furthermore, at the time of writing, the Dental Board of Australia has released a draft Scope of Practice Registration Standard and Guidelines which if accepted, will see the scope of practice of dental auxiliaries expanded, to encroach on the range of services typically offered by general dentists.[3]

The upshot is an unprecedented oversupply of dental professionals in the marketplace. Under normal circumstances, some of this excess could be absorbed into the workforce as older dentists retire. However, as a result of the GFC, many of the older dentists have seen their retirement savings take a hit and are no longer in a position to retire in the time-frame that they imagined. The end result is a glut of dentists and dental auxiliaries.

The situation is so extreme that a prominent dental benchmarking firm predicted that as at March 2013, there may have been up to 1200-1500 unemployed dentists nationwide;[2] a situation that in the past would have been beyond comprehension.

This structural shift in the dental profession has occurred against the backdrop of the largest economic shock the world has seen since the Great Depression. Not only do we have a massive oversupply of dentists, we're also seeing a sharp decline in the demand for services as patients concerned about their own financial futures have come to see their dental spending as discretionary rather than as a necessary health service. Treatment that was once accepted, is now deferred or replaced by a cheaper alternative.

A study conducted by Insight Economics (commissioned by the Australian Dental Association) into the relationship between supply and demand states: "The point is that the supply of dentists is expanding at a rate well in excess of the rate of population growth. Unless per capita demand for dental services expands strongly a surplus of dentists will emerge given unchanged trends."[4]

The simple truth is that these studies bear out what many dentists at the coalface reported anecdotally some time ago.

2. Concentration of Ownership

The last decade has seen a massive concentration of practice ownership as corporate raiders buy up dental practices all over the country. There are several larger players in the industry, each with their own unique business model.

What they do have in common is that they will be the main beneficiaries of the glut of dentists. These companies regard the oversupply of dentists and dental auxiliaries as a source of cheap labour, and there has already been considerable downward pressure on dental wages, with an increased emphasis on providing a return for the shareholders. For every dentist not willing to work under such conditions, there will always be some who are.

3. Increased Influence of Medical Insurance Companies

Medical insurance companies are also making their presence felt in a variety of different ways. Their initial foray into the market was through the introduction of preferred provider schemes. In return for providing dental services at an agreed rate, insurance companies agreed to refer their policyholders to participating practices, thus providing an additional source of patients for those practices.

However, some dental practices that signed up for these schemes stopped taking responsibility for generating their own patient flow. When practices become more and more dependent on the medical insurance companies for patients, they are vulnerable to having the terms of any agreement dictated to them – and changed as the insurance companies see fit.

In the past, when the insurance company decided to reduce the fees paid to dentists for a given service, most dentists complied out of concern that their patient base would leave en masse. Consequently, dentists needed to see more and more patients just to make ends meet. This model may well work from the actuarial perspective of the insurance companies, but many doubt it is suited to optimising patient outcomes.

Some medical insurance companies are also opening their own branded practices. They are aggressively marketing these directly to the public in an attempt to lure patients to their surgeries with the promise of lower fees or no-gap dentistry.

It would appear that these multinationals want to compete on every level of dentistry: this was emphatically shown when one of the largest players, Dental Corporation, was purchased by BUPA, a large British medical insurer.

It is unclear exactly how events will unfold but what has become clear is that practices which originally sold to Dental Corporation are now working directly for a medical insurance company. Under the original sale agreement, practitioners were required to maintain a particular level of profitability for a specified term (usually five years). Once this obligation has been met, and the requirement to maintain this level of profitability has been fulfilled, other business models may be employed.

The core business of medical insurance companies is insurance, not providing dental services. It seems logical that one option for BUPA will be to use their network of dental practices to drive the uptake of medical insurance policies. The question in the minds of some commentators is whether or not Dental Corporation practices become a massive, preferred-provider network for BUPA to facilitate that outcome (subject to regulatory compliance). If that occurs, what is the fate of those preferred providers not under the umbrella of Dental Corporation?

Medical insurance companies and other corporations have not yet begun to flex their muscles. These companies have deep pockets and big marketing budgets. When they do make their presence felt, you will see intense competition and price-driven dentistry as the various corporations look to increase market share.

4. Medical and Dental Tourism

Another trend affecting the fortunes of dentists in Australia is the rise of dental tourism.

In difficult economic times, this option can become more attractive to a price-sensitive public. The fact that patients can have a holiday thrown in, makes the proposition even more enticing.

I dare say most of us would have had a patient or two go to South East Asia to have their dental treatment completed at a lower cost. What many dentists don't realise is that medical and dental tourism is a $100 billion industry globally, which over the coming years is expected to grow at a rate of 8-9% per annum. Australians reportedly have approximately $300 million of medical and dental procedures performed overseas each year.[5]

For the first time, Australian dentists face significant competition from overseas. Although the challenges with having dental treatment overseas are numerous, the trend for patients to seek low-cost alternatives is here to stay.

Dentistry is a highly-regulated profession in Australia. These regulations provide many consumer safeguards, such as high-quality training, national registration, mandatory professional development and stringent infection control. All of these safeguards come at a cost which is ultimately passed on to consumers.

Where there is less regulation, there will be less cost. There will also be fewer consumer safeguards in place. A significant concern relates to the quality of the treatment provided and like most dentists, I have seen patients return from these trips where treatment has failed catastrophically.

When treatment does fail, there is the issue of how a warranty is fulfilled. Many local dentists have found themselves in the situation of trying to rectify a problem that was not of their creation. Rectification treatment can be more extensive, challenging and ultimately, more expensive than the initial treatment. If the patient returns to their overseas dentists, there are logistical challenges relating to travel and timeliness of remedial treatment to overcome.

Until recently, patients wanting dental treatment overseas had to make enquiries through a travel agent or through their own efforts. However, it was recently reported that NIB, a major medical insurance company in Australia, has decided to actively promote a medical tourism-based business model to its network of policy-holders.[5] They argue that they have overcome the challenges associated with quality control and warranty and expect to sell over 1,000 packages in their first year of operation at an average price of $8,000 per package.[5] In effect, NIB is now actively competing with Australian dentists – even those practitioners who helped them establish a market presence through their preferred provider scheme.

Rather than bleat about a lack of loyalty, we need to remember that NIB has taken the action it feels is in the best interests of its shareholders. The lesson for all of us is to understand that large corporations will always behave in this manner. It's not personal, it's just business – to them at least.

What Does the Future Hold?

No-one has a crystal ball that can predict the future with complete certainty. What we do know is that dentists are facing business conditions never seen before. These conditions continue to change and it's likely we have seen only the tip of the iceberg.

Many dentists are already finding it harder-than-ever-before to run a profitable practice, but most of the new graduates and dental-auxiliaries are yet to enter the profession. We're in for a bumpy ride and there is only one certainty – a business-as-usual approach just won't cut it. We're going to see a Darwinian approach to dental practice – the survival of the fittest.

We are currently seeing, as a result of increased competition, that dentists are finding it more difficult to attract new patients as well as retain existing patients. Coupled with a fragile economic sentiment and the fact that patients are generally more inclined to shop around (without a compelling reason to do otherwise) to compare the prices of dental services, many dentists are struggling to maintain profitability. Dentists are rightly concerned about their future.

Dentists in traditional private practices are under threat. For these practices to remain viable, dentists need to be able to compete in the marketplace and provide a compelling reason for patients to come to them rather than to clinics run by corporations or medical insurance companies.

The big advantage is that dentistry is a relationship-based business. Smaller, boutique practices are better positioned to offer a more personalised experience than large corporations. The marketplace is still in a state of flux and smaller practices, if nimble and with the right approach, have an opportunity to outperform the larger corporations in this critical area of business.

Won't the Government Save Me?

In Australia, successive Federal Governments don't have a fantastic track record of rolling out dental programs. For instance, the Chronic Disease Dental Scheme (CDDS) was a mixed blessing for the profession. While such programs offered a source of revenue for dentists during turbulent economic times, administrative compliance was poorly articulated and burdensome. Because the program was not means-tested, there were many people receiving subsidised dental care who could afford to pay their own way. Inevitably, there were cost blowouts and one method of recovery was to impose extraordinarily punitive measures for minor administrative breaches. What's more, some dental practices had become so dependent on this program as a source of revenue, that when the program was abruptly cancelled, they went broke.

Governments of all persuasions are concerned with what they perceive is in the best interest of the electorate (not to mention their own political fortunes). Because their mandate is to govern for the country as a whole, their desire to look after a particular profession may be limited, particularly when advocacy for the profession can easily be dismissed as a vested interest.

The dental profession has a proud history of acting in the interests of public health. It was this profession which took the principled stand of urging the politicians to fluoridate water supplies that reduced the prevalence of dental caries. The sustainability of a profession and professional standards deserves to be on the national agenda as much as access and affordability of dental care. In the absence of strong advocacy on this issue, the dental profession runs the risk of being turned into a mega commercial enterprise, owned by a handful of players whose interests are not necessarily aligned with the profession or that of the national interest.

The current oversupply of dentists has been caused by decisions taken by successive Governments. However, as Einstein said, "we cannot solve our problems with the same level of thinking that created them." It is hard to believe that those who caused the problems have the political will or capacity to correct them.

Waiting for some sort of government life-line is surrendering the significant power we have as individuals to create our own lives. So, it is up to each dental practitioner to forge their own path and to secure their own prosperity.

Why Traditional Marketing Won't Work

Our patients are consumers in many other areas of life. They are constantly bombarded with marketing whether it be for electrical goods, holidays or anyone else trying to grab their attention.

We live in a world where marketing is ever present. You need only look at how department stores design their marketing calendar, promoting one festivity after another to see that consumers are constantly bombarded with such messages. It is little wonder that consumers, including our patients, begin to tune out.

The mistake many dentists make is that their marketing is trying to compete in the noise of the general marketplace. The marketing messages put forth by most dentists are of the "me-too," vanilla-type messages that are heard everywhere and lack cut-through. This is partly due to the fact that the advertising guidelines published by the Dental Board of Australia, have been crafted in such a way as to limit the use of certain marketing practices. While the consumer protection sentiment of the guidelines is admirable, the guidelines themselves do restrict the use of legitimate marketing initiatives such as testimonials.

However, the boring marketing messages published by most dentists is also related to the reluctance of dentists to express their point of difference. Many dentists with whom I have discussed marketing, have told me this reluctance stems from concerns about how they'll be perceived by their peers.

According to economic researchers Adriani and Deidda, "The ability of sellers endowed with high quality goods to inform buyers about the quality of their goods could be crucial in keeping these sellers from being wiped out by price competition."[6]

I believe there is a place for effective external marketing in an overall marketing plan. However, a lack of either opportunity or willingness to inform buyers of the quality of their services, will mean the limited return on investment will not warrant the expenditure.

Without a relationship to draw upon or a point of difference to be explained, dentistry becomes just another homogenous commodity being flogged to consumers. When dentistry is commoditised, inevitably comparisons are made on price. To understand the effects of commoditisation and price-driven dentistry, you need only look at the effect it has had on other industries and professions.

What I have observed (and research supports this too) is that once a service becomes commoditised (as a result of excess capacity and a lack of differentiation),[8] many businesses respond by reducing prices in an attempt to attract more customers. And for a while, it works. It works until a competitor reduces their prices even further, sparking a price war.

We have seen this time and again in various industries such as the supermarket industry, the milk industry, and the airlines. Large corporations become the price-makers, while smaller operators become price-takers. They compete for a while, but without the economies of scale, diminishing margins see many smaller businesses ultimately fail.

There is a segment of the population that will always make decisions based primarily on price. During uncertain economic times more people examine their expenditure and look to save money wherever possible. Under these circumstances, slick marketing can increase the proportion of the market making their healthcare decisions around price. Smaller practices run the risk of being dwarfed by larger operators as dentistry continues to become more commoditised: as demonstrably occurred in the supermarket industry.

So, in competitive times, relying on external marketing initiatives to sustain and grow your practice is fraught with danger. Not only are you advertising to "cold" prospects – those with whom you have no relationship – you are competing in a very noisy, competitive and price-driven market-place. Traditional marketing alone just won't work.

I prefer a more predictable approach, based on existing relationships where I don't have to constantly be chasing new business, and patients happily pay what we ask for our services.

A Note to Specialists

As the general economic times become more challenging and competition increases, there is a tendency for general practitioners (GP's) to look after their own needs and keep as much work in-house as possible. They do this by looking to expand their scope of services and therefore refer less to specialists.

This, of course, can be challenging for specialists as there can be a reduction in patient-flow and the work that is referred tends to be technically difficult. Additionally, many specialists have reported they have seen an uptick in "rescue" jobs as some general practitioners have over-reached in an attempt to keep the work in-house.

Just as general dentists need to adapt to changing times, so too must specialists. Where in the past referrals could be assumed, they must now be earned and continue to be earned. Where a practice may have simply relied on referral as the primary source of patient flow, many are now marketing directly to the public – in essence competing with their referral network.

Customer retention is a core activity common to successful businesses, irrespective of the industry. As the dental profession continues to evolve, the need for specialists to create a strong network of referring practitioners will increase dramatically, irrespective of other marketing initiatives.

A referral from a colleague is a much easier sale, because the specialist is able to trade off the relationship the patient has with the referring dentist, resulting in a shorter sales cycle and, significantly greater case acceptance.

No-one can predict the future with complete accuracy. However, what we do know is that no matter what the economic environment is like, creating, supporting and growing a strong referral network makes good business sense.

2

PATIENT RETENTION, THE NEW BLACK

The purpose of business
is to create a customer.

—

Peter Drucker

PATIENT RETENTION, THE NEW BLACK

The only way for dentists to not only survive – but thrive – in difficult times is to have a core group of patients who continue to support our practice, a group which comes to us even when it is easier or cheaper to see someone else.

However, in recent years the dental profession has been caught in a perfect storm. Making a living as a dentist is harder than it has ever been and is set to get harder still. As a profession, we are entering uncharted waters.

Building a practice in good times is easy – patients are plentiful and have money to spend. If patients leave, they are easily replaced – easy come, easy go – but good times do not last.

It is your patients who will support you through the difficult times. Our job is to give them a reason to want to do so.

By taking on the challenge of building a practice of loyal patients in difficult times, you will have created the foundation for massive growth as circumstances improve.

Retention vs Loyalty

The aim of this book is to help dentists retain their patient base in the face of competition. Before I proceed any further, I want to discuss the difference between retention and loyalty.

Retention, as its name indicates, is concerned primarily with keeping patients in the practice, irrespective of the means used to deliver that outcome. Loyalty, on the other hand, implies a sense of attachment to the practice by the patient. A sense of loyalty is fostered through engagement with the patient and through creating a relationship with them.

This book is primarily concerned with helping you build a practice that will sustain you over decades. We're taking a long-term view here. If you want a sustainable practice, aim for patient retention through loyalty.

As you read through the book, where I refer to retention, retention through loyalty is implied unless otherwise stated. I will deal with loyalty programs as a separate issue.

The Benefits of Patient Retention

Patient retention makes good sense from an economic, professional and emotional perspective.

In lean economic times, there is often a huge push by practices to acquire more new patients. While the need for increasing patient flow is understandable, often there is little attention given to actively nurturing relationships with existing patients.

What many dentists have failed to realise is that retaining your existing patients is not only the best way to withstand the upcoming competitive challenges, it also provides a platform from which to grow the practice.

Patient retention is the bedrock of a successful practice.

There are four primary reasons why the best customer is the one you've already got.

1. Cost Effectiveness

Acquiring a new patient is typically more expensive than retaining an existing one. This is especially true if the practice undertakes external marketing campaigns such as search engine marketing, search engine optimisation, social media advertising and radio or newspaper advertising.

The astute reader will point out that word-of-mouth marketing (covered in a later chapter) is a virtually free way of increasing patient flow and they'd be right. However, the foundation of word-of-mouth advertising is a patient who is happy to recommend the practice to others. The more happy patients within the practice, the faster word-of-mouth advertising can grow your patient base.

2. Improved Personal Satisfaction

Perhaps one of the most satisfying aspects of being a dentist is getting to spend time with other people. Nearly all of the dentists I speak to rate this as one of the most rewarding aspects of the profession.

Over time, you and your patients go through life together and as relationships deepen, you get to share in life events to an extent – some patients may even become friends. On a personal and a professional level, it is really gratifying to know your patients care for your well-being as much as you care for theirs.

3. Improved Professional Satisfaction

At the same time, you become more than just a dentist to the patient: you become a trusted advisor. As a trusted advisor, patients are far more likely to stay at the practice because they want your guidance when it comes to dental health. With a long-term relationship, you are also better to offer continuity of care and plan for the future needs of the patients as well as phasing treatment over time.

4. Improved Financial Performance

As the trusted advisor you are better able to propose more comprehensive treatment and as a result of your relationship with the patient, you are more likely to have that treatment accepted. Improved case-acceptance will not only improve the health and well-being of our patients but also improves the financial health of the practice.

Patient retention is a win-win-win. It fosters stable relationships with patients which is a win for the patient, by virtue of improved patient care. It is a win for the dentist because it allows them to practise the type of dentistry they enjoy on patients whom they like. Lastly, patient retention is a win for the practice: due to improved business stability, increased revenue and decreased marketing costs.

If dentists can master the art of retaining their patients, they will enjoy a rewarding career and never need to engage in costly marketing again.

Why Retention is More Crucial Than Ever Before

Today, patient retention is more crucial than it has ever been. In the boom times, patients come and go. There is a plentiful supply of punters ready and willing to engage our services. So when a patient leaves, it is no big deal – there will be others to replace them.

However, during recessionary times, the demand for dental services (and others) diminishes significantly. Coupled with increased competitive pressure as a result of an over-supply of dentists, many practices find themselves with holes in their appointment books.

A wise colleague once told me that when everyone is earning enough money, there is a sense of egalitarianism within the profession. However, as soon as people begin to feel the financial pinch, our survival instincts are activated and self-interest comes to the fore.

I have previously indicated that other than the dentists themselves, the number one asset of a dental practice is the patient base because it represents predictability and stability of earnings.

Earnings stability and predictability, of course, affects the profitability of the practice, which in turn affects the lifestyle a practice owner enjoys: what school your children attend; what holidays you take; what sort of superannuation you have, and so on.

What's more, profit and its inherent predictability contributes to the saleability of the asset when a dentist comes to retire. From a purchaser's perspective, a practice with a stable patient base is a less risky proposition than one where the patient base is uncertain. Practices with stable and predictable earnings are clearly more valuable than practices with a history of erratic earnings.

While there is no doubt the general economy will recover from its current malaise, it is expected that the dental economy will remain fragile for many years to come. This, of course, is due to the fact that until the oversupply of dentists washes through the system and equilibrium returns, the profession will experience a sustained period of intense competition. As the number of dentists (and auxiliaries) continues to rise, competition for the (relatively) finite number of patients will continue to increase. Your patients will be marketed to by many other dentists in an attempt to lure them away.

Ultimately, it will be those practices that manage to retain and grow their patient-base that flourish into the future. Practices that don't, will struggle and may even fold.

If dentists are to continue to enjoy a satisfying quality of life and a secure retirement, patient retention must be a priority.

A Note to Specialists

Although this chapter has dealt with the retention of patients, the same concepts hold true for the retention of any client.

As I mentioned in the previous chapter, specialists serve two clients: the first is, of course, the patients themselves and the second (assuming the patient has been referred) is the referring practitioner – be that a general practitioner or another specialist colleague.

For many specialists, marketing directly to the public will be an integral part of an overarching marketing plan. However, one of the common elements of successful specialist practices is that the practitioners have developed, and continue to nurture, a core group of referring practitioners.

Developing a strong referral network will become increasingly important for specialists as competition in dentistry continues to increase. For, as competition increases, it is expected that general dentists will refer less, and will look to provide as much treatment as possible in their own practices. So for specialists, developing a strong referral network remains critically important.

The benefits of retaining a referral-base are just the same as those of retaining a patient-base: cost effectiveness; improved personal and professional satisfaction; as well as the improved financial performance of your practice.

Clearly, for specialists to operate a successful practice, most will need to develop strategies to retain patients as well as their network of referring practitioners. The principles outlined in the following chapters apply to both groups.

3

THE POWER OF "WHY"

The two most important
days in your life are
the day you are born and
the day you find out why.

—

Mark Twain

THE POWER OF "WHY"

There are some leaders and companies that truly inspire: they create a movement, they're different and they change things. How is it that these inspired companies and leaders create a following where others do not?

Author, Simon Sinek, informs us that inspired leaders and companies think, act and communicate from a place of vision – they attract people to their vision.[7]

He argues that customers don't buy what you do but why you do it. His research indicates that all the insanely successful companies and great leaders in the world think, act and communicate in this same way and it is exactly the opposite from how everyone else does it.

Every single person or organisation knows what they do. Some know how they do it; whether it be a unique selling proposition or some other proprietary methodology. However, very few know why they do what they do. When I say why, I don't mean making a profit. Profit is not a reason for a company to exist, it simply represents how well that company has performed.

While it is true that some companies that don't communicate their purpose do experience commercial success, the companies that are founded on a larger "why" are always more memorable and more successful because of it.

So what is your vision for your practice? Why is it that you do what you do, and what is your calling? Are you simply going through the motions, or is your dentistry an expression of a higher purpose?

Why in Action

When I talk to dentists about purpose and vision, some feel it is a bit "woo-woo" and doesn't relate to the bottom line. However, purpose-driven businesses are not only more profitable but also more fulfilling for those in them.

Whether it be a company or a social movement, communicating your "why" and what you believe will attract a following of people who believe what you believe.

For a practice to reach its potential, it is important to understand that the aim is not to do business with every single person, but the mission is to attract and retain ideal patients – those who believe what you believe.

Understanding one's purpose is at the very core of a successful business, as it is in life. Let's look at a few examples of people and businesses who live their "why". You can judge their success for yourself.

Apple

There is no doubt that Apple has had phenomenal success as a company. It is regarded as one of the most innovative companies and its customers (me included) are raving fans.

One reason that Apple has been so incredibly successful is that it has clearly articulated its "why" or vision, and set about attracting people who bought into that vision as well. Apple's core value is the belief that people with passion can change the world for the better. Apple's own tagline, "Think Different" tells us that its "why" is to challenge the status quo in all it does.

As the driving force behind Apple, Steve Jobs set about building a company with that vision as its centrepiece. Apple expresses that vision by making beautifully designed computers that are simple and easy to use.

That vision has contributed to Apple having a market capitalisation of over $450 billion.

Rosa Parks and Martin Luther King Jr

In 1955 Rosa Parks, an African American woman, was arrested for not giving up her bus seat for a white woman as the law of the time dictated.

Her arrest sparked the Montgomery Bus Boycott and was a pivotal moment in the Civil Rights Movement in the United States. Rosa's arrest galvanised supporters of the National Association for the Advancement of Coloured People, including a new minister in town – Dr Martin Luther-King Jr.

The struggles and triumphs of the Civil Rights Movement are well-documented. But how did one woman's act of defiance lead to sweeping changes, not just in the United States, but across the world? Did it take courage? It sure did. Hard work? Persistence? Passion? Yes, yes and yes.

But it all started with a dream. A dream crystallised by Rosa Parks and communicated so eloquently by Martin Luther King in his "I Have a Dream" speech.

Dr King was not the only civil rights activist at the time. However, the clarity and power of his vision energised a nation and changed the course of history. Fifty years after it was delivered, his message of equality still resonates.

Zappos

Another company that thinks, acts and communicates from the point-of-view of their vision is Zappos.com. Zappos is the world's largest online retailer of shoes with annual turnover in excess of $1 billion dollars. In 2009, it was acquired by Amazon in a deal also worth over a billion dollars.

Zappos is known for its legendary customer service. Their raison d'etre is to deliver happiness, and how they achieve this is by providing an exceptional customer experience when their customers buy shoes. As CEO, Tony Hseih says, Zappos is not in the business of selling shoes but rather the business of making people happy.[8]

The common element between these extraordinarily successful enterprises is the clarity and communication of their "why". This is what initially attracted and continues to attract large numbers of people to these businesses – people who share a similar world view. This alignment of values is what creates loyalty beyond rational explanation.

If you have never experienced this, go and stand outside an Apple store before the launch of the latest iPhone, iPod or iPad. There you will see as loyal a band of followers as you'll ever see anywhere on the planet. The common element? They believe what Apple believes.

Discovering Your "Why"

Discovering your "why" sounds like an easy thing to do, right? Go and sit cross-legged under a tree, meditate for an hour or so and, hey presto! There it is!

Sure, some people just "get" their "why", almost osmotically, as they travel through life. However, for most people, years of conditioning, taking on responsibilities and dealing with what's urgent means their core purpose is buried deep inside.

Many people feel a lack of purpose and energy in their lives. Outwardly, they're perceived as successful. However, many mistake achievement for success. Have you ever achieved a goal and felt, "Is that it?" The missing ingredient is fulfilment. Fulfilment is an art and is intrinsically related to operating from your "why". For most people, uncovering their "why" takes some time, effort and reflection.

Discovering your "why" is a process. It involves examining your life to determine those times you felt lit up, energised, connected and in flow. It requires digging deeper and finding common threads in different areas of your life, over different stages of your life, when the world made most sense to you.

Writing a journal is a useful tool to record your thoughts and feelings as you go through the exercise of learning about yourself. The key to effective journal writing is to ask yourself quality questions. Here are a few to get you started:

- What did you love to do when you were young? What did you want to do when you grew up? Why?

- Who were your favourite teachers at school? What was so great about them? Be specific.

- What do you love to do today? What activities cause you to lose track of time? This is called being in flow.

- What are you naturally good at? What do others see as your strengths? What help do others ask of you?

- Has there been a specific holiday or event you've enjoyed? What specifically did you love about it?

- If time and money were no object, what would you really do with your life? Sure, most of us would spend some time sunning ourselves in the tropics. But the novelty would soon wear off. And then what? What would you do if you were free from responsibility? Allow yourself to dream along with this question.

If your rational brain is interjecting with, "Yeah but," then follow up by asking yourself, "Why is that important to me?" This allows you to better uncover the emotion behind the answer.

Sinek says that you'll know you're getting close to your "why" when you have a visceral response such as goosebumps or the hairs standing up on the back of your neck. Often, it is hard to describe the feeling in words. That's because the response is coming from the limbic brain – that part of the brain incapable of language but responsible for feelings, as well as gut instinct and intuition.

By its very nature, this journey is a deeply personal one. I have found it has taken several iterations to determine my "why". Like everyone else, I found it hard to articulate my "why" – to give language to these feelings that arise from the limbic brain.

As I examined the different stages of my life, my "why" seemed to evolve as my life evolved and changed. I found it puzzling that my internal compass seemed to point in different directions at different stages of my life. I struggled with this for ages until I realised I had confused my "why" with the "how" and the "what".

I discovered that my "why" is to build or be a part of groups of people whose company I enjoy and feel energised and stimulated by.

This has shown up in my life as a boarding school student, a dentist in the Navy, a husband and father, a member of various business groups that I belong to and, of course, in my practice.

I discovered that a practice is merely a vehicle that brings my cause to life.

In my practice, this has manifested by creating a team that has a genuine family spirit; one in which we all care for one another. We understand how we all contribute to the patient experience and we all strive to support other team members in their roles. Do we get this right one hundred percent of the time? Of course not. We're human. We make mistakes. But each day we re-commit to playing our best game.

The same principles hold true for our patients. Rather than building a group of patients, we have tried to build a group of friends. We have striven to create an environment where we can enjoy one another's company. For us, this has taken on as much importance as providing excellent clinical care and has, in turn, provided a huge dividend in terms of happiness and fulfilment. It turns out that operating from our vision is also good for business.

Action Steps

1. Complete the journal exercise in the chapter.

2. Once you have articulated your "why", look at your practice and see if it is giving life to your purpose.

3. How can you bring your "why" into your practice so that you attract and retain more of your ideal type of patients?

4. Examine all aspects of your life to see where you are congruent or incongruent with your life's purpose or "why".

Download the Workbook

Remember to download the companion workbook to access checklists, cheat sheets and other resources. It is available at:

www.drjessegreen.com/retention/workbook

4

STAY WITH ME

The key to this business
is personal relationships.

The Late, Great, Dicky Fox.

—

Jerry Maguire 1996

STAY WITH ME

A key feature of successful practices is the creation and maintenance of a large enough group of patients who continue to frequent the practice, accept treatment, pay their bills and refer others. How do successful practices achieve this? By creating compelling reasons for patients to do so.

In the past, being a good dentist was enough to create a profitable practice with strong patient flow. However, these days that is just not the case.

There is no doubt that good clinical dentistry is an essential component to a successful practice. Treatment that consistently fails leads to a breakdown in the patients' trust in the individual practitioner and the practice. Because loyalty cannot exist in the absence of trust, frequent episodes of treatment failure will lead to patient loss.

However, being a good or even a great dentist does not guarantee a successful practice – it is merely the entry price – and from here on in, it is assumed.

So, if clinical dentistry alone is not the key to creating a reason for patients to stay, then what is? The answer lies in creating a reason for patients to stay – a reason so compelling that patients will walk past other, more convenient, lower-priced practices to visit you.

This chapter will outline the 4 essential elements required to create a compelling reason for patients to stay:

1. The Importance of Relationships

2. Loyalty and Trust

3. Building Value

4. The Power of Community

I will also discuss loyalty programs and their use as a tactic for patient retention when loyalty has not yet been established, at the end of the chapter.

1. The Importance of Relationships

Relationships are the glue that holds society together. The quality of our relationships determines the quality of our lives. This is as true for our business life as it is for our personal life. Taking the time to invest in relationships with our patients helps create a sustainable, profitable and enjoyable business.

How Do You Expedite the Process?

While there are no short cuts to developing relationships, you can create an environment more conducive to forming relationships. According to behavioural expert Allan Pease, the secret lies in understanding that "questions are the answer."[9] That's why part of my new patient examination process is dedicated to conducting what is officially known as a pre-clinical interview but what I call a "fireside chat". The purpose of this conversation is to get to know as much about the patient as I can, in as short a time as possible. Initially, I enquire about their chief complaint, dental history and dental aspirations.

However, I try to find out as much about them personally as I can too – what they do for a living, where they work, whether they have holiday plans and what hobbies or interests they have.

So that I can deliver the best possible care to the patient, I'm looking to understand what motivated them to make their appointment in the first place, and what, if any, concerns they have regarding their dental visits.

Building Relationships in Action

Information provided by patients during their 'fireside chat' is recorded by the dental assistant (DA) in the patient file. We are very open about the fact that we record the information. I begin the conversation by mentioning that as we speak, my DA will take some notes so that all the important information is captured accurately.

Typically, the conversation may start with something like:

Me: "Mrs Smith, so that I can get to know you better and understand more about your dental history and what's important to you, I wanted to spend the first fifteen minutes or so of the appointment having a conversation with you. Is that OK with you?"

Mrs Smith: "Sure, no problem"

Me: "Before we start, I want to introduce you to my assistant, Tina, who's going to take some notes in the background. That way, we can record all the pertinent information accurately. So, you might hear the keyboard a little as we talk. Is that OK?"

Mrs Smith: "That's fine."

Using the Information

One of our internal communication systems is to have a short meeting at the start of every day. I was first exposed to this as a dentist in the Navy and, over the years, it has also served me well in private practice. The meeting allows us to choreograph our day and the experience the patient has with us. From my perspective, the meeting is like receiving a briefing and as part of that process, I am reminded of little details that might otherwise escape my mind.

Some dentists have a fantastic memory and can recall every pertinent patient detail without ever having to make notes. I must admit that I just can't remember that much information without prompts. What's more, my staff may not (yet) have the same relationship with the patient as I do. So it is important that we have a process for the sharing of relevant information amongst the team with a view to optimising the patient's experience at our practice.

As an example, I am reminded of patients such as Mr Baker who works at ABC Corporation and whose daughter, Mary, had a baby boy, whom they named John, in December 2013. When I see Mr Smith during the day, I will be sure to enquire after baby John and Mary.

Is this choreographed? For sure. Am I genuinely interested in this patient? Absolutely. Does writing notes detract from my good intentions? No way.

We see many, many patients throughout the year and it is impossible to remember every detail about each of their lives. Writing notes as a memory jogger simply ensures we get the details correct.

Relationships Between Staff and Patients

I know some dentists who guard their relationship with a patient. Some even become jealous when another team-member develops a relationship with *"their"* patient.

From the perspective of patient retention, it is critical that staff are empowered to develop their own relationship with the patient. In larger businesses, the talk is about the principle of *"more of our people engaging with more of their people."*

When a patient has a relationship with only one staff member in the practice, it represents a single point of failure. If that staff member moves on, the patients' relationship with the practice can be severed, ultimately resulting in the loss of the patient. Practices with patients whose relationship is primarily with an assistant dentist, oral health therapists or hygienist, are most vulnerable in this regard.

When relationships are formed between multiple staff members and the patient, the bond between the practice and the patient is strengthened such that if a staff member does leave, the patient is more than likely to stay with the practice.

An additional advantage of empowering the staff in this way is that they then become more engaged in their work and tend to stay on longer. Assuming you hired well at the outset, staff longevity increases productivity (as they become more familiar with their job) and also reduces the training burden and upheaval associated with staff turnover.

Compromise

Dr Stephen R. Covey, the author of the bestselling, *"7 Habits"* books,[10] is credited for popularising the concept of an "emotional bank account." The concept is essentially, that to nurture loving relationships we need to make as many deposits into this account as possible, so in the event of a withdrawal we have enough to cover it.

The simplest way to make deposits into the emotional bank account is to take a genuine interest in others. Withdrawals include staff appearing unhelpful, indifferent, uncaring or overly rigid in the application of practice policies.

Relationships are dynamic and there will be occasions when the practice makes compromises for the sake of the relationship. The same holds true for our personal relationships. It's OK to yield a little to preserve the relationship and when you yield a little, the patient will too.

The key is to understand two things: what you are willing to compromise on and what you're not willing to compromise on.

How to Maintain Relationships through Communication

Maintaining a relationship is like tending a garden. Just like a garden, a relationship needs care, attention and nourishment to keep it alive. When neglected it withers, stops yielding fruit and if weeds (competition) take hold, the relationship may ultimately fail.

So what is required to nourish a relationship? Communication.

Communication has been described as a contact sport – so do it early and often.[30]

High Tech vs High Touch Communication

In today's digital world, communicating is easier and cheaper than it has ever been. Yet paradoxically, communication has become shorter, more abbreviated, and increasingly perfunctory with the advent of these technologies.

There is little doubt that technology assists in delivering communication very easily. The mistake many people and businesses make is that they assume that because the mode of delivery has become faster-paced, the communication between the practice and the patient can be abbreviated. In so doing however, communication becomes transactional rather than being used to nurture the relationship – the very opposite of what is intended.

How many times have you called a bank or a phone company to resolve an issue only to face an endless cycle of computerised menus, when all you really want to do is to talk to a real, live, human being to help sort it out? I know that when I need to call these businesses, I often feel frustrated by the depersonalised experience and I'm left feeling that I'm treated as a number rather than a valued customer.

It's important to remember that technology is just a method of delivery and should not compromise the feeling of caring that accompanies the message being delivered.

In our practice, we employ a range of technologies to deliver our communication pieces. However, we aim to keep our communication as "high touch" as possible.

For that reason, we don't use SMS reminders and the like. I prefer our patients to hear from our receptionist, whose voice they have got to know and trust. I like to use this touch-point as a means of enquiring about our patients' wellbeing and deepening the relationship.

What I found when I was working in practices that employed SMS reminders was that cancellations and no-shows were higher than when a patient spoke directly to a staff member, especially if they had met. It is much easier to say no via text rather than having to speak to a person. Other dentists I speak to report similar findings.

When I explain my philosophy about not using SMS to dentists, many feel I'm being inefficient with time or that I'm a luddite of some sort. It has been my experience that the time invested in these sorts of calls has paid dividends many, many times greater than the small investment of time it takes to actually make the call.

Types of Communication

I like to remain in regular contact with patients and we have scheduled methods of communication. Some of the more obvious ones include recall letters, appointment confirmations, post-operative care calls, birthday acknowledgements and referral thanks. In our practice, these are definitely "high touch" occasions and are done via telephone, or by hand-written card.

However, I also like to supplement routine communication with other forms of communication such as newsletters, blogs, emails and social media. These are forms of mass communication and are best delivered digitally.

With all of these forms of supplemental communication, it is important to stick to your own editorial guidelines rather than wandering off on tangential subjects.

A. Newsletters

There is nothing new in publishing a practice newsletter. It is a tried and true method of communicating with your patient base at regular intervals. In the past, newsletters were printed as a hard copy before being mailed (at great expense) to patients.

There will be patients who still prefer a hard copy, but for those who prefer an electronic copy, emailing the newsletter as a PDF is, in my opinion, perfectly reasonable.

Keep the subjects as interesting and as varied as you can. Sometimes, you can provide a synopsis, in lay terms, of recent developments in the dental literature. At other times, you might like to write a human-interest story about a staff member or a cause you might support. You're only limited by your imagination. But do keep your readers in mind, and aim to add value with each successive newsletter.

B. Blogs

Writing a regular blog is also a great way to remain in contact with your patients. Patients can subscribe to it via a RSS feed or email. Once posted, the blog will find its way into your patients' inbox where they can read more about your philosophy of care or other topical matters.

Although blogs are typically written, they can be posted as an audio file or a video. Different people prefer different formats, so you should feel free to mix them up a bit.

Once your audience is tuning into your blog, keep the frequency of blogging consistent. Your audience will come to expect the blog on a certain day.

(As an aside, regular blogging also helps improve search engine ranking for your website if the blog is constructed properly.)

C. Email Marketing

Email marketing is especially useful for communicating with those who are yet to become patients of the practice. Not all visitors to a website will become patients immediately. So, unless we have their contact details, we have no way of contacting them and they disappear back into the black hole of cyberspace. Collecting details is especially important if we have paid for web traffic via pay per click advertising because having an opportunity to initiate contact with the visitor, means they may potentially become a patient, thus improving the return on investment (ROI).

The process of obtaining a visitor's contact details is typically achieved by a process called "opting-in". In this process, a visitor to a web page will enter their name and email address so that they can download a report or other digital product. These details are stored in an auto-responder (such as Mailchimp, iContact or Aweber) and we are able to email these visitors and begin the process of developing a relationship with them before they even set foot in the practice.

We have all been customers or potential customers ourselves so it is important to remember to treat these people the way we'd like to be treated ourselves. The purpose of these email messages is to genuinely establish a relationship and add value in whatever way we can. If we have done our job well and invested in a relationship without pushing ourselves upon them, we will be front of mind when the time comes for them to seek dental treatment.

Used well, email marketing can take a whole lot of potential patients and covert them into actual patients.

D. Social Media – Friends with Benefits

Word-of-mouth is still the most common way people express their likes and dislikes, and is the way people generally communicate with their friends and relatives. Social media is simply word-of-mouth on an electronic platform.

Social Media has been a mainstream way of communicating for several years now. There is no doubt that it is here to stay and that it's a very useful tool in a dentist's marketing plan.

While many of my contemporaries dismiss it or just don't want to know anything about social media, it's important for those with similar views to understand that even though they may not want to participate, most of their patients are using social media to engage with their friends and networks. Using social media is a legitimate method for creating and nurturing relationships with patients.

None of this will be new to the younger generation who has grown up with social media as par for the course.

There are many different social media platforms, including Facebook, Twitter, Pinterest, Google+, Instagram, YouTube and LinkedIn.

A complete breakdown on each social media platform and the intricacies of each is beyond the scope of this book. For the tech-heads interested in learning the mechanics of social media, I can recommend *Social Media for Dentists 2.0* by Jason Lipscombe and Stephen Knight.

Social media has many applications in dentistry. In the context of developing relationships, social media is used to interact with your patients. Like the name says, social media – is social. Communication is a two-way street. So it is imperative you are prepared to engage with your patients and not just broadcast at them from your social media platform.

Take Facebook for example: it is a straight-forward exercise to post a status update or to have your blog feed into your News Feed. The key, of course, is to build an audience with which to interact.

Building an Audience

There are many strategies in doing this. The primary one is to encourage your patients to "Like" your page so that your status updates automatically go into their news feed.

There are innumerable ways to get clients to "Like" your Facebook page. You're only limited by your imagination. Here are five simple ways to get you started.

i. Put Your Facebook Page Address on Everything

Promote your Facebook page (and other social media platforms) on all your marketing collateral – business cards, letterhead, practice brochures, procedure information sheets, newsletter, email signature and so on.

Be sure to utilise the customised URL because it is a better branding for your business and is easier for patients to remember.

ii. Encourage Twitter Followers to Come Across to Your Facebook Page.

On Facebook, you will obviously be able to share more content in a more comprehensive way than is possible on Twitter. It is worth making the effort to bring Twitter followers across to Facebook so that they can learn more about you and the practice.

iii. Give Incentives for People to "Like" You.

You can be as creative as you like here. Perhaps you want to run a competition and to enter, participants need to "Like" the page. Alternatively, you could offer a downloadable document where part of the download process requires the visitor to Like your page. (This is a twist on the opt-in strategy for email marketing).

iv. Join Groups

Groups are very powerful. Groups on Facebook are like forums. When a question is asked in a group environment, where possible, try to answer that question in a manner that adds value without expecting anything in return. By continually adding value you will be positioning yourself as a trusted expert in this area. It is better to interact in this area using your personal Facebook account because it allows you to add value without the perception of acting solely for commercial gain. It also allows you to build your personal brand. By interacting with groups through your own profile, you will ultimately attract more people to your profile (where your work details should be displayed) and ultimately, more patients.

v. Ask People to "Like" Your Facebook Page.

Have all of your staff post a status update on their personal page asking their network to come across to the business page and "Like" it.

Try not to make these requests too frequently. Once a week or fortnight is sufficient. You can even be a bit cheeky and mention that this is your regular fortnightly-status update asking friends to come and Like your business page. Have a little bit of fun and let your personality shine through.

When posting a status update, be smart. Make sure it has something interesting and compelling to entice people across to the business page. This avoids the appearance of being "spammy".

Checking In

Facebook can also be used for patients to let their friends know they see you as a dentist. This is achieved when they "check-in". By "checking-in" at your practice, your patients are broadcasting to their network that they receive their dental care at your practice. In effect, they're endorsing you.

Creating Communities

The joy of social media is that it's very good at helping to create a sense of community about the practice. The practice becomes a focal point of interaction and discussion.

Another application of Facebook is to create a closed or secret group. Closed groups are set up to be visible to the public as a possible group to join, but only members can see what has been posted in the group. Secret groups, on the other hand, are set up so that they're not visible to the public at all.

You might choose to invite all your patients into a group so it takes on the feeling of a "club" – building a sense of community and belonging. This is a place where additional information can be provided to existing patients that might not be readily made available to the public. For instance, it could be a chance to share personal news items perhaps, of the team at the practice, or it could be a forum to post handy hints on certain topics and generate discussion around those hints.

Closed and secret groups can also be used as a method of creating an "Advisory Board" – a select group of patients from whom the practice might seek advice and commentary about how to best improve the patient experience at their practice. These boards may meet face-to-face periodically but could interact in this group environment.

What About Complaints?

Be aware that some patients may use social media as a platform to make a complaint. Many dentists whom I know are concerned about patients airing their grievances publicly. I take a different view. If a patient has a grievance, I'd prefer to know about it and resolve it. If a patient vents on social media, at least I can respond rather than having them leave the practice and vent to other people without my knowing or having the right of reply.

Social media is here to stay and its applications are only limited by your imagination. Having a policy of creating engagement with your patient-base through social media is an essential element of a patient retention strategy.

Disclaimer: The use of social media by dentists in Australia is governed by the Guidelines for Advertising of Regulated Health Services published by the Australian Health Practitioner Regulation Agency (AHPRA). Commentary provided in this book is of a general nature and the AHPRA guidelines should be adhered to at all times. If you have specific questions regarding compliance with the above regulations, you should seek a legal opinion.

2. Loyalty and Trust

One of the single most important factors affecting patient loyalty is trust.

If relationships are the glue that holds society together, then trust is at the heart of the relationship. Trust is also the mother of loyalty.

Trust is a fragile commodity that can take years to develop, can be broken in a heartbeat and can take an eternity to repair. In the absence of trust, relationships are unsustainable – it's as simple as that.

So what is trust and how can it be engendered and maintained?

While researching this book it became apparent that both the meaning of trust, as well as the symbols of trust, differ from person-to-person and it is because of this that authors describing models of trust examine at length factors affecting trust.

After reading numerous books on the topic[11,12] I found that the factors affecting trust could be broken down into three broad groups: Ability, Behaviour and Character – the ABCs of Trust. There is of course an interrelationship between behaviour and character.

Dr. Covey's son, Stephen M. R Covey, makes the point in his book *The Speed of Trust*,[11] that the concept of an emotional bank account holds true for trust as well. This, of course, gives rise to the question of what constitutes a deposit into or a withdrawal from the Trust Bank (TB). He also points out that trust is a two-way street, and although in this book we're primarily dealing with ways to enhance a patient's trust in the dentist and practice, it's equally important for the practice to trust the patient in return.

Let's have a closer look at the ABC's of trust and their effect on the trust bank account balance.

Ability

I have mentioned previously that being a good dentist is in itself not enough to guarantee a successful practice. However, it is clearly an essential element of a successful practice because predictable clinical outcomes provide certainty for patients, and certainty is a basic human need.

Successful treatment outcomes represent a deposit into the trust bank account and provide patients with a sense of certainty and confidence in the dentist. By comparison, repeated clinical failures represent multiple withdrawals from the trust bank account and can lead to patients neither trusting the clinical judgement of the dentist nor his ability to perform treatment to a satisfactory standard.

Anyone who has been in clinical practice long enough understands that there are times when treatment fails even if it has been performed with the best intentions and to a high standard. There are a myriad of reasons why this could occur. The key is to be able to predict and communicate the possibility of failure before it occurs. When potential problems are predicted and communicated ahead of time, trust is maintained. However, trust is broken when a failure occurs that has not been predicted or worse, when failure comes after extravagant predictions of a glorious success.

Behaviour

The second element of trust relates to our behaviour: our deeds must match our words and intentions. There are many specific behaviours that relate to trust. Rather than detailing each behaviour, I want to discuss three broad aspects of behaviour that relate to trust.

The first aspect of behaviour that influences trust is whether or not our behaviour is congruent with what we say for what we do is just as important as what we say.

Some time ago, my daughter's class was presenting its work at the school assembly. For a reason that escapes me now, I was unable to attend the assembly. Later that night, when I tucked her into bed and told her that I loved her, she replied, "No you don't." I was completely surprised to hear her say this and even more so when she used my non-attendance as evidence for her hypothesis. It was only then that I realised my behaviour had not been congruent with my words. Although I had been expressing my love for her verbally, my actions communicated to her, a lack of caring for her.

The issue I had with my daughter related to what she perceived as a lack of congruence between my words and my deeds. My deeds (or lack thereof) meant more to her than any words of affirmation.

Such examples of incongruence are easy to spot. But congruence is in the eye of the beholder and what may seem congruent to us may seem incongruent to others. For example, I know a dermatologist who is so busy that he can't cope with more patients. He doesn't take on new patients because he is committed to providing the best level of care he can for his existing patients. When new patients call they are simply turned away. I know this to be true because I have been a patient at the practice and received excellent care. Yet when my daughter needed an appointment she was turned away. He feels he is acting congruently with his desire to provide a high level of care for his existing patients.

The issue is that his mission statement and core values revolve around improving the well-being of all people. So how is this incongruence resolved? Does he change his values? Does he work 24/7 and burn himself out? Perhaps one way to resolve the incongruence is to be able to refer new patients to another practice where they can receive care. Referring patients on means that the dermatologist doesn't suffer the effects of burnout and by offering patients assistance with a referral to another practice, he fulfils his values of helping all people.

Like the dermatologist, we may be behaving in a manner that appears incongruent to patients yet we're blissfully unaware we're making a withdrawal from the trust bank account.

Our behaviour must not only be congruent with our words but also with our values. When our behaviour is incongruent with our values, not only is trust diminished in the eyes of others, it is diminished within ourselves as well.

The second aspect of behaviour that relates to building trust is to behave in a consistent manner. We all know people who run hot and cold – their behaviour can vary from one day to the next. Although such people may be perfectly pleasant, it becomes difficult to rely on them if their behaviour changes with the wind. This lack of reliability makes it hard for others to interact with them with any sense of confidence. As such, a lack of consistency in behaviour is a trust-buster. On the other hand, consistent behaviour imparts a sense of certainty and predictability about behaviour. By behaving in a consistent manner, others will be comfortable knowing where you stand, and being reliable allows others to be able to depend on you and contributes to a positive balance in the trust bank account.

The third aspect of behaviour that builds trust is to behave in a manner that demonstrates a caring attitude. Author John Maxwell has a saying that *"people don't care how much you know until they know how much you care."*[13] We're in a people business and our whole business is caring for our patients.

All religions have an equivalent to the Christian saying *"Do for others what you want them to do for you"* (Matthew 7:12) The simplest way to build trust and continually make deposits into the account is to treat others as you would want to be treated yourself – it really is as simple as that. Remember, we're all customers at other businesses so we know how we like to be treated.

A very rapid way to break trust with patients is to appear uncaring or indifferent to their circumstances. That doesn't mean we need to accede to every request made of us, but we do need to deal with patients from an empathetic perspective and find a way to meet their needs within the framework of the practice's needs.

Character

Character has been defined as the sum of qualities shown in a person or group. It is who you are and it guides your decisions and actions throughout life. In conjunction with ability, character is at the core of a person's credibility.

A key component of character is integrity. Integrity refers to the consistent adherence to a moral code or set of values. These values may include qualities such honesty, loyalty, compassion and care

Clearly, the consistent adherence to these principles informs behaviours and actions. Adopting a virtuous set of values and consistently adhering to them will be a trust-builder of the highest magnitude and contributes to a healthy Trust Bank Balance.

As the trust bank balance grows, relationships with patients deepen and the loyalty a patient feels towards the practice (and indeed the loyalty the practice feels for a patient) increases. However, with trust comes responsibility. Patients won't always know if you're doing the right thing when you're treating them. When it comes to creating and maintaining a patient base, the importance of creating an environment where trust is fostered cannot be underestimated.

3. The Importance of Building Value

Patients will only value what you do as much as you value it yourself. If we, as dentists, are continually downplaying what we do for patients, it is only natural that patients will too.

Perhaps the greatest enemy of "loyal" is "satisfied". Satisfied means that the patient's expectations were met and they got what they paid for. Satisfied patients don't refer new patients abundantly. It is only by creating a group of loyal patients that you build a strong platform for practice growth.

When patients are "satisfied", the relationship is more transactional in nature rather than being based on loyalty. They were not "Wowed" in any way. Consequently, these patients are vulnerable to making decisions regarding dentistry based on price. They're also susceptible to being lured to another dental practice through canny marketing or a recommendation from a friend loyal to another dentist.

Why is it important to build and communicate the value we offer patients? Is it simply to blow our own trumpets? Not at all.

The purpose of building value is three-fold:

i. The first reason for communicating the value you offer is to position yourself as the trusted advisor. A trusted advisor is regarded as an expert in their field and is there to help guide the patient through the various stages of their dental life.

   As I discussed in the previous chapter, trust must be earned through ability, behaviour and character.

   By communicating the value of treatment, you are demonstrating your diagnostic and treatment-planning abilities as well as a genuine concern for the well-being of the patient – behaviour and character.

   When this process occurs in the context of a developing relationship, patients come to view their dentist as their trusted advisor and loyalty is engendered.

ii. A second reason for building value is that by impressing upon the patient the importance of dental treatment, they make it a priority in their life.

   Although it is rarely communicated in this way, most failures to attend and no shows occur because the patient simply got a better offer. In other words the circumstances of the patient changed and something else took priority over their dental treatment.

   So by raising the level of awareness about the value of dental treatment and making it more of a priority in the life of the patient, it is not only less likely that the patient will cancel or not show up but also ensures that they get the treatment that they need.

iii. Thirdly, building value also reduces the barrier to case acceptance. There are many reasons why patients elect not to proceed with treatment. One of the most common objections is that they can't afford it. While that is genuinely true in some instances, the more common reason is that they don't see enough value in it to justify the expense. As dentistry becomes increasingly commoditised, many view it as discretionary spending. So when making the decision about whether or not to proceed with treatment, it is not always viewed through the prism of a health-related decision but as a discretionary expense along with other items such as kitchen renovations and overseas trips. I think we'd all agree that there is a component of discretionary spending to dentistry hence we must elevate the importance of dental care in the eyes of the patient.

Again, by adding value for what treatment has been completed and what is yet to be done, the patient begins to value their dental health more thus giving it a higher priority.

Communicating Value

To effectively build value, it needs to be communicated before, during and after each appointment.

Before the appointment commences, I aim to impress upon the patient the importance of the upcoming treatment. I explain to the patient what we are doing and why it is important.

For instance, I might say: *"Mrs. Jones, today we are going to be replacing a large filling in the upper left first molar. There is some new decay under the existing filling that if left untreated, could lead to pain or even the tooth fracturing."*

During the procedure, I continue to talk to my patients, explaining what I am doing (where the patient is receptive to these discussions). In the scenario I described above, I would let the patient know that the cavity is large and that it is lucky that we're restoring it before it gets any worse. I would then re-iterate the consequences that would probably occur if we left it. The conversation might sound something like this:

"Mrs Jones, the hole in this molar tooth is really deep. The good news is that the decay hasn't yet reached the nerve of the tooth, although it is very close to it. I'm really glad we got to it when we did because had we left it, you would almost certainly have needed a root canal therapy. By getting to it now, we have given the tooth the best chance of avoiding those dramas."

After the procedure has been completed and I am debriefing the patient, I will re-state the same message. *"You did very well today Mrs Jones. That was a big job. Although the decay didn't quite reach the nerve I expect the tooth to be a bit tender for a few days. Had we left it any longer, I think the tooth would have needed a root canal treatment. Although there is a possibility the tooth may still require one, we have given it the best possible chance of avoiding one."*

And when I get to reception after the appointment I debrief the receptionist: *"Charlie, Mrs Jones has done very well today. We did a really big filling for her on the upper left first molar. We got to it in the nick of time but I think it will be tender for a few days. Can we please give her a call to see how well she's going?"*

Am I saying all this for the receptionist's benefit? Not at all. Charlie, my receptionist, can see from the item numbers in the computer what treatment was completed. I am simply having this conversation with Charlie in front of the patient to reinforce what was done in the appointment and the resultant benefits.

If Mrs Jones had further treatment that needed to be completed, I would follow up with: *"Mrs Jones, you have another hole on the lower right molar. After today, I'm concerned that if we leave it any longer, we might not be as lucky as we were today." Then I turn to Charlie and say "Charlie, can you please arrange my schedule so that I can attend to the lower right molar for Mrs Jones as a matter of priority. We need to get that done before it causes any further problems."*

These conversations have served multiple purposes. Firstly, it lets Mrs Jones know that she's lucky that we restored the first tooth when we did and that it was a big job. By stressing to her the size of the task several times, it lowers her resistance to the upcoming bill.

Secondly, we have warned her that the tooth may need further treatment and lastly, we have built value for the next visit by letting her know she has other issues which, if left untreated, could be very problematic. We have used today's treatment to confer a degree of urgency for the outstanding treatment.

If Mrs Jones did not have any further treatment that needed to be completed, we would look to build value for the next recall examination instead. So after the initial conversation with the receptionist we might follow up by saying something like:

"Mrs Jones, you don't need any more dental dramas. So that we can ensure any problems are dealt with early, easily and conservatively, I'd really like to see you in September (i.e. six months' time) for your preventive maintenance examination. Cavities can develop pretty quickly and I'm concerned that if we leave it any longer we're running the risk of seeing more cavities like the one we had today. I'm going to ask Charlie to schedule an appointment for you and at least then it is in the diary. If circumstances change, we'll handle that. It's important this doesn't fall through the cracks."

Many years ago, I had a distribution business and a mentor of mine taught me that the purpose of an appointment is to have another appointment. That lesson has stuck with me and I have applied it to the way I run my practice. Patients will always leave with either an appointment to return or if they can't commit to a time, permission to later contact them to schedule a time. We have a structured system in place that even lets us book recalls six months ahead with virtually no cancellations or no shows. It also allows the patient to plan ahead for appointments for other personal needs.

Our entire system of positioning, reducing no shows, reducing fee objections, increasing case acceptance and providing the best level of care has been built on the foundation of demonstrating and communicating the value we offer to patients. It is one of the core skills you and your staff need to master if you want to move from having satisfied patients to having loyal patients who pay their bills, come back to the practice and also refer their family and friends to your practice.

4. Power of Community

The paradox of the modern world is that as we become more connected in some ways, we become more isolated in others. According to a recent study, the prevalence of loneliness in all age groups is increasing in contemporary western society. One of the factors affecting the vulnerability to, or the protection from loneliness, is the quality and quantity of social interaction. Researcher, Brené Brown, concludes that an irreducible need of men, women and children is that of love and connection.[14] Other researchers have found that happy people have a strong social network.[15]

Building Community

Recently, I was having a conversation with a group of women and one of the women, who was new to town, asked for a recommendation for a hairdresser. I found the discussion really interesting because I didn't fully understand just how attached some women are to their hairdresser.

I found that that one of the reasons these women enjoy going to their hairdressers is the social nature of the appointment and the sense of community around the salon. Was this cultivated deliberately or was it just a happy accident? I was curious to find an answer to this question and so I went and spoke to some hairdressers to find out the answers.

When I spoke to the hairdressers and discussed what I had learned, they were not in the least surprised. One of the hairdressers said to me that she felt her role was as much that of counsellor and confidante as it was a hairdresser. She has been cutting hair for nearly twenty years and told me that over time, most of her clients had become friends – not in a way where they would socialise beyond the salon – but in a way that it felt like catching up with old friends each time they arrived for a haircut.

When it came to creating a connection and a sense of community around the salon, while the hairdressers acknowledged that it had occurred, it seemed to have occurred spontaneously.

Why Do People Like Being Part of a Community?

Each one of us is a member of multiple communities, ranging from family groups to neighbourhoods, sporting clubs, churches and so on.

Belonging to a strong and supportive community that nurtures positive relationships imparts feelings of a sense of belonging, resilience and security, through access to a peer-group and its associated support. Critically, in mature communities, that care becomes bi-directional, with the individual members caring for the community they are a part of as much as the community cares for them.

Being a member of a given community leads to shared experiences that foster the development of community norms and builds cohesiveness within that community.

Dental Practices and Community

One of the serendipitous consequences of building authentic relationships based on care and trust, is that over time patients begin to see the practice, in part, as their broader community. As their connection with the practice deepens, patients feel a sense of belonging to something bigger. The result is that they have a vested interest in the well-being of the practice in general.

Recently, a client of mine celebrated twenty-five years in practice. To celebrate, the practice held a party and invited many of its long-standing patients. Although the event was ostensibly to celebrate the longevity of the practice and its principal, it actually ended up being a celebration of the people in the community who happened to share the same dentist – their dental family. Patients mingled with each other and the members of the practice team, creating their own moments of connection. The feedback from the event was fantastic with many patients commenting on how much they enjoyed being a part of the dental family. My client came to realise just how much his patients cared for him and how important the practice was in their lives.

Loyalty Programs

I am often asked by dentists whether or not there is a place for loyalty programs in their practice. Loyalty is first and foremost related to the strength of the relationship between the practice and the patient – nothing can trump that. In the absence of a meaningful engagement with a patient, the practice cannot hope to retain patients.

Most "loyalty programs" as we traditionally know them are really short-term promotions that are designed to get repeat business. While I can see that there is place to drive sales and retain patients, however, "loyalty programs" aim to buy loyalty rather than earn it. There is a difference and it matters.

However, if patient-flow is really slow, there is a place for "loyalty programs" in a dental practice. While they don't replace the need for establishing and maintaining relationships that engender true loyalty, they are a useful adjunct to assist in patient retention. As competition in the dental profession increases over the next few years, having another string to the patient retention bow could prove very useful. It is important for practices to recognise the difference between retention and loyalty as they roll out such programs, while simultaneously aiming to develop deeper relationships and engagement with the patient to engender true loyalty.

Loyalty programs that I suggest for dentists are not the type normally employed by food outlets. There are other, more elegant incentives you can offer patients to remain at the practice.

I believe that we must add value to the lives of our patients in every interaction we have with them. When designing a loyalty program, it must answer the question, "How can I enrich the life of my patient?" By approaching the program from this perspective, the end result will resonate as a natural thing for the practice to do rather than some gimmick aimed at hooking patients into the practice.

If the programs are well designed, add value to the patient, and are well executed, they can play a pivotal role in retaining patients.

Below are some examples of how you can use loyalty programs in your practice to drive patient flow and assist in retention.

A. White Teeth For Life

The concept of this program is that patients who elect to whiten their teeth are offered the opportunity to maintain their white teeth by receiving top up bleaching provided that the patient returns for their routine examination and continued bleaching remains appropriate.

This program is primarily aimed at ensuring that patients keep their scheduled recall examination appointment.

B. Patient Appreciation Events

Patient Appreciation Events represent an opportunity for the practice to not only thank their patients for their custom but also represent an opportunity to foster loyalty by deepening relationships and creating a sense of community.

There are many variations of the Patient Appreciation Event, but my preferred one is to turn the event into a community service if possible. In that way, the practice is able to have a positive impact on the wider community.

For instance some of my clients have held an event where they offered training in cardio-pulmonary resuscitation (CPR). The practice had to complete CPR training anyway, so figured they might as well invite their patients along too. They hired a venue, organised a first aid company to deliver the CPR training and provided some light refreshments on the day.

By all accounts it was a huge success. The patients really loved the fact that they had learned a new skill and it was a talking point in the local community. It also created the sense of community amongst the patients with the dental practice as the hub. The feedback from the practice was that the staff also felt enriched by the experience. By offering CPR training for patients, they had performed a community service that certainly added value and might just save a life.

C. Corporate Loyalty Programs

Some of my clients have developed a loyalty program in partnership with companies such as accounting firms or law firms. The basic premise of their relationship is that there is an inducement, such as a discount, on routine services for the staff and family members of that particular company, provided that regular examinations are maintained. The discount is not necessarily extended to all services.

D. Strategic Partnerships

One of the keys to developing successful practices is developing robust partnerships with other businesses that have customers similar to our ideal patient but where there is no competitive overlap. Strategic partnerships are not loyalty programs per se, but they are a close relative and worthy of mentioning here.

When choosing a potential partner it is important to look at who is in your network and determine who already has a great reputation, who already has a great product or service that is pleasing to their customers and who has access to large numbers of people in your target market.

You may package your products and services together and launch co-branded initiatives or you may simply act as referral partners for one another's businesses. You're only limited by your imagination.

Initially, you're trading off the loyalty the patient has with your strategic partner. However, as your relationship with the patient deepens, they will begin to feel a sense of loyalty to your practice, independent of any relationship they have with your strategic partner.

Action Steps

1. Examine what processes you have in place to gather information from patients, how it is recorded and how you can use this information to develop a deeper understanding of who they are what motivates them.

2. Determine the occasions you want to communicate with your patients and classify these contacts as high-tech or high-touch. You may want to consider:

   - Creating a quarterly newsletter

   - Creating an information product for prospective patients and linking this to an autoresponder. Follow up with an email sequence that provides information of genuine value to readers.

   - Blogging regularly and linking this to your practice's social media platforms such as Facebook.

3. Examine the ABCs of trust. Look at ways you can add to the trust bank account and plug any leaks from it.

4. Own the value you provide to patients and develop a system of communicating it in an elegant fashion to them.

5. Begin the process of creating a community with your practice at the centre.

6. Understand the difference between loyalty and loyalty programs. Where necessary, implement loyalty programs to aid patient retention.

Download the Workbook

Remember to download the companion workbook to access checklists, cheat sheets and other resources. It is available at:
www.drjessegreen.com/retention/workbook

5

CUSTOMER EXPERIENCE

Do what you do so well that they will want to see it again and bring their friends.

—

Walt Disney

CUSTOMER EXPERIENCE

I have said it before, but I will say it again: being a great dentist is important but it doesn't guarantee a successful practice.

Patients can't judge the quality of our technical work. Unless it's really bad, they can't determine how well their crown fits or the anatomy you place in a posterior composite restoration. What patients do however, is use proxies to judge how good a dentist you are in their mind. The thing they notice above all else is how well they felt they were cared for.

Therefore, we need to create a customer experience around the parameters patients can judge and what is important to them rather than only what is important to us from a technical standpoint.

The concept of great customer service seems so passé these days. Go to any bookstore and there are an endless number of books on the subject. It seems everyone understands the need to provide customers with a great experience.

So why is a great customer experience so rare and why is customer service in general, so bad? I bet that if I asked you to recall your last bad customer service experience you would not have to think too far back.

Despite a mountain of readily available information on the topic, poor customer service is the norm.

Businesses such as Apple, Virgin and Disney are renowned for providing a fabulous service experience. They're hailed as trailblazers and pioneers in the field, and they are. What is it that sets them apart from other businesses whose customer service is less than exemplary?

There are two primary reasons most businesses fail to succeed in the way Apple, Virgin and Disney have. The first is a lack of visionary leadership. The best leaders create a vision for their business and communicate it in such a manner that it inspires their workforce. To borrow Simon Sinek's phrase, they start with "Why?"

The customer experience doesn't happen by accident it is created with specific intent. Whether it is Steve Jobs designing the Apple Store, Richard Branson hamming it up on a Virgin flight or the "cast members" greeting you at Disneyland, your experience is choreographed from the very beginning and nothing is left to chance.

You don't need to be Steve Jobs, Richard Branson or Walt Disney. You just need to have a vision of the experience you want to create for your patients. The vision must excite you enough so that you want to talk about it. Inspired employees are passionate and energetic. Without passionate and energetic employees there is no hope the business can deliver an outstanding customer experience.

The second reason most businesses fail to deliver exceptional customer service is that they lack the skills to deliver it. Thankfully, the skills required to deliver a great customer experience can be learned. And like all skills, the more your team practises them, the better they get.

Little Things Make a Big Difference

It has been said that excellence is the result of doing a lot of little things well. Excellence is not an accident but is the result of a deliberate and persistent effort.

Committing to the habit of excellence on a daily basis ensures a continual focus on providing an exceptional patient experience that consists of a series of "Wow" moments.

"Wow" moments are those when the patient is surprised and delighted by the service they receive at your practice. In a service-based profession such as dentistry, these moments typically represent moments of connection between the patient and your practice.

To create such moments, we need to choreograph the patient experience from their first interaction with the practice to their last. Much as the director of a dance or film would plan the routine or scene, we need to plan the patient experience from start to finish. By planning the patient experience, we can create an environment that encourages moments of connection and we can demonstrate a genuine desire to serve the patient at each of the touch-points (e.g. incoming phone calls, greeting the patient, handing over the patient from the dentist to another staff member, etc.) in the practice. Once you have your "routine" planned out, the staff can then overlay their passion, enthusiasm and personality. We call this process "systemising and then humanising".

There are many touch-points in a dental practice and we need to choreograph the ideal experience our patients should have at each of them.

Five Service Standards

How is it that businesses like the ones we discussed earlier Apple, Virgin and Disney are able to consistently deliver such a great customer experience that their brand is renowned for it?

As I have discussed, the answer lies in having a clear and vivid vision for what customer experience they want to create looks like and then choreographing it so that by the process of repetition, the customer experience becomes systemised and the default way of operating.

Choreographing a customer experience involves developing an overarching set of service standards and examining how to apply these standards in a practical way at each interaction that a customer has with the business. You can follow the same process for your dental practice.

In a moment, I am going to outline my Five Service Standards. What I'd like you to do is to write down and examine each touch-point in your practice and rate yourself on each of these five criteria. Once you have rated yourself you will certainly identify areas for improvement. The next step is to ask what you can say or do better in each of these areas and come up with a plan to improve.

If you apply these service standards to each touch-point in your practice, it won't be long before you're giving your patients a great story to tell about your practice. Not only will your patients be fiercely loyal, but they won't be able to help but tell others how wonderful you made them feel.

1. The Name Game

There is nothing more musical to the human ear than one's own name. That's why the first Service Standard is to greet people by their name whenever possible.

Obviously, it will be easier to greet those patients you know by name already, rather than those you don't. However, in most practices it is quite easy to know which patient is due to arrive at any given time.

By keeping up-to-date records, you will know their name, their gender, and their age before they arrive. From there, it is generally safe to make an educated guess and say, *"Hello, you must be Mr. Smith. My name is Mary. I've been speaking with you on the telephone."*

Let's have a look at an example of this Service Standard in action.

I really don't like shopping for clothes. In fact, I will do just about anything to avoid it. I find the whole process quite tedious, though the problem of course is that over time clothes wear out and need to be replaced.

I lived in Canberra from 2002 until I sold my first practice in 2008. During that time I came across a great menswear shop called "Blades Menswear". The clothes were attractive, but quite expensive. Those who know me will understand that I'm not known for my love of fashion. So why did I go there? I went there because the staff knew how much I loathed shopping and essentially, dressed me. They chose what looked good and steered me away from items that didn't suit me. It was the only place I shopped and all the sales assistants knew me.

Fast forward to March 2013. I had just moved back to Canberra and was due to speak at a conference in Hong Kong. My wardrobe was looking old and tired. (I don't think I updated it during my five-year absence!) I was departing the next day and I needed some new jeans to take with me.

I walked into Blades, not expecting anyone to recognise me – I was wrong. The owner of the shop, Rodney, immediately came and greeted me. *"Hi Jesse, how are you? We haven't seen you for ages. Where have you been?"* I was really impressed that he had remembered me.

After a brief discussion about what I'd been up to in the intervening time, I told him I needed a pair of jeans in a hurry. Not only did he remember my name, he remembered styles I liked and disliked, as well as my size. I explained to Rodney that I was in a hurry so he arranged for the jeans to be hemmed within the hour.

I was so impressed that after a five-year absence, Rodney and his staff not only remembered me but also were interested in what I had been doing during those past five years. The relationship had endured and I purchased two pairs of jeans. But more than that, I didn't and still don't go anywhere else for clothes! I am a raving fan.

2. Be Present

Buddhists have a saying *"be where your feet are"*. So often when we go about our day-to-day activities, our minds are elsewhere. If we want our patients to experience a sense of connection with our practice and feel noticeably cared for, then our attention must be in that moment.

Have you ever been engaged in a conversation with someone but they seemed miles away? Did it feel as though what you were saying was important to them? When you're not in the moment and dealing with other people, the risk is that you are perceived as being uninterested and uncaring.

Dental practices are busy places. Phones ring regularly and there is an endless array of tasks to be completed. However, we need to remember our purpose: to create a practice of happy patients who pay, stay and refer others. Being present creates space for truly meaningful interactions and developing deeper relationships.

Possibly the worst example of not being present I have ever experienced was at an appointment with a shoulder surgeon to whom I had been referred. By reputation, he was one of the best in the country and was the "shoulder guy" for many of the elite national sporting teams.

When I arrived at the practice, I was greeted by a surly nurse who told me to take a seat in the very large waiting room and wait until I was called. After a while, another nurse appeared at the opposite end of the waiting room and called out my name. Before I could approach her she had turned on her heel and was marching up the corridor. She neither greeted me nor introduced herself.

I was instructed to remove my shirt and to sit on the examination bed in the middle of the room. The doctor would be in shortly, I was told. The nurse left, leaving the door open with me in a state of partial undress and feeling a little exposed and uncomfortable.

When the doctor did arrive, he didn't introduce himself either – at least not until I directly asked his name after introducing myself. He quickly examined my shoulder and then perused the x-rays I had brought with me.

After an examination that lasted literally less than five minutes, he advised me that I needed surgery and that I should return to the reception to make the appropriate appointments. He turned and was about to walk out when I piped up and asked a few questions. He seemed irritated by the fact that I wanted to ask questions before my proposed surgery.

After my questions were answered, he left the room – again leaving the door open as I was trying to dress myself. He'd also left all my x-rays and other images either on the x-ray viewer or scattered on the adjacent desk. I gathered them up after I had hurriedly dressed myself.

I actually had the intention of booking the appointments but when I returned to the reception desk, the receptionist was on the telephone for what seemed like an eternity without acknowledging that I was waiting.

In the end, I had to leave because I had to get back to work. I have never experienced service as bad as that from a health professional. I would not have believed service could be as bad as that had I not experienced it personally. Perhaps the doctor was so busy he didn't feel the need to care about or be polite to his patients. I really can't explain it.

That surgeon lost me as a patient purely because of his dismissive attitude and poor service. He was never engaged with me or interested in my concerns. He did not even stop to ask what I did for a living and how the surgery might impact on that. He seemed to forget that there was a person attached to the shoulder. One thing is for sure, I have never felt more like a "number" than I did that day.

In the end it was a lucky escape for me because after a lot of physiotherapy and yoga, my shoulder has remained untouched by a scalpel. I wonder how many other patients he has lost? The truth is that we will never know – and neither will he!

3. Yes

The popular television program *"Little Britain"* has a famous skit about terrible customer service in which "the computer says no". Wouldn't it be terrific if instead of being told "no", customers could be told "yes" instead?

When a customer makes a request they are looking for a solution, not a heap of excuses about why their request can't be accommodated. Words are very powerful and customer-service expert, Jeffery Gitomer, suggests starting sentences with phrases that give the customer what they want.[16]

> "The simplest way to deal with that..."
> "The fastest way to get that done is..."
> "The best way to handle that is..."

So if a patient breaks a tooth and telephones asking for an urgent appointment, the receptionist focuses entirely on what the patient is saying to ensure she is "present" and listens intently. She might then respond by saying something like *"Oh, Mr Smith, that's terrible. The best way to handle this is to make an appointment to see Dr Green on Friday. I know he'll be keen to sort this out for you."* We have now been able to accommodate the patient and maintain the practice's schedule.

Just remember that we're all customers somewhere. How would we want our requests handled?

4. Plus One

The Rule of Plus One involves discovering our patients' service expectations and then doing at least one thing to exceed them. With Plus One, you create an opportunity for multiple moments of connection in the overall patient-experience. When you really "wow" customers, you give them a great story to tell and a reason for them to recommend your services.

Let me give you an example: I love coffee. I love everything about it: the smell; the flavour; spending time with friends; the ritual of drinking it – everything.

Wherever I live, I like to find a great café. When I lived in Brisbane, my café of choice was Espresso Republic located in Gresham Lane in the CBD. Now that I live in Canberra, I like to have coffee at Koko Black, which is a bit odd, because it is a chocolate shop.

I love both of these cafés for exactly the same reasons: the first is that the coffee is consistently good; the second reason is that the staff at each café know me and my order and they make my coffee how I like it. The staff look for ways to "plus one" me in different ways at different times. Whether it is by giving me a chocolate or simply farewelling me in a way that makes me want to come back, both café managed to make my day better for the experience.

Imagine the experience your patients would have if you applied The Rule of Plus One at each touch-point in the practice. Your patients will have a huge "WOW" experience and will truly love your practice.

5. Have Fun!

Have fun! It may seem a little at odds with the notion of being present but having fun or being playful energises your team. Let's face it, not many of our patients come to see us because they think it will be a fun outing.

Having fun means taking what we do seriously but not taking ourselves quite so seriously in the process. Having fun at work is not just a frivolous pursuit – it has serious benefits for the bottom line too.

Having fun and being playful at work creates an environment where patients feel more relaxed at a time when they might otherwise feel more anxious. When patients walk into our practice they can feel the vibe of the place, and if everyone is grumpy, tense or stressed, it is hardly conducive to creating a great customer experience. If we can engage our patients with a sense of fun, the relationship between the patient and the practice deepens and the loyalty patients feel towards the practice increases.

However, there is also evidence that creating happiness in the workplace leads to increased productivity, creativity and a willingness to go that extra mile for patients. Happy employees tend to stay in their role longer, meaning that the costs associated with staff turnover, in terms of training and decreased productivity, are avoided.

Having fun is integral to our enjoyment of life in general. We spend a lot of time at work so it pays dividends – personally and professionally – to incorporate a sense of fun and playfulness in our interactions with patients and staff alike.

Dental practices are not normally renowned for being fun places to be. So the concept of having fun might, at first, seem at odds with dental treatment. In fact, when I have mentioned the concept of having fun to some dentists, they express the concern that dental care might be trivialised.

Having fun does not mean professionalism should be abandoned at the first opportunity. Although we take what we do very seriously, we don't take ourselves too seriously as we strive to "make" our patients' day.

Fun at our practice usually takes the form of banter. Although we do like to laugh, we're still very much present and in the moment. While we aim to improve the happiness of all with whom we come into contact through fun, we do have a major rule of engagement – never say anything that could offend anyone – period.

Fun doesn't necessarily have to be demonstrated as banter. Clearly, each team will create a sense of fun that works for them. For instance, I know a practice that creates a sense of fun through the use of magic tricks. Patients of that practice love it and eagerly await their next appointment to see what magic trick the dentist/magician will perform for them next.

It doesn't really matter how you choose to have fun. Just keep it simple and be authentic.

Introducing fun into the practice pays huge social and emotional dividends through team harmony, that is, creating an environment where the experience is as valued as the treatment performed. Ultimately, introducing fun leads to happier workplaces, improved professional satisfaction and improved relationships with the team as well as with the patients.

Delivering WOW!

Applying these service standards at the different touch-points within the practice provides the framework for choreographing the patient-experience.

It also allows us to systemise moments of connection with our patients that form the core of their experience with us. Systemising the patient experience ensures that the level of care is consistent, no matter which staff are rostered on any particular day. Once the system is in place, staff can overlay their own personality – systemising and then humanising.

The end result is that the culmination of a lot of little things leaves the patient feeling truly cared for and in wonderment. "Wow! How do they manage to do that when other businesses don't?"

Once you have begun to "Wow" your patients, it is important to realise that you have set a new benchmark or norm for them. Soon enough, patients come to expect your great service and are less in awe of it.

In order to consistently surprise and delight patients, you need to regularly review and improve your systems. Examine each of the touch-points in your practice and look at how to apply your Service Standards to them in new ways.

What's the Story?

Whether you like it or not, patients have a story about your practice that they tell their family and friends. The story might be positive, neutral or negative – you don't know. Obviously, we want our patients to be advocates for our practice and the best way to do that is to give them a great story to tell.

By consciously creating an environment that gives patients a great story to tell, you are more in control of the message they take out into the world and how your practice is perceived in the marketplace.

A great customer experience is the foundation for word-of-mouth marketing. Giving your patients a great experience and story to tell not only ensures your patients stay at the practice, but that they become flag bearers for the practice and refer their family and friends to it.

Good News

Truly great customer service is rare these days – even "good" service is not so common. It seems poor service has become the norm. All you need to do is to spend time dealing with one of the major banks or telecommunications companies and you'll know this to be true.

Like most people, I have encountered many examples of poor customer service from companies who refer to themselves as service-based industries. In a way I'm grateful for their lousy service because people's service expectations have been lowered to such an extent, that it really does not take much to surprise and delight patients.

As you begin to implement strategies for enhancing the patient experience, you will notice you don't have to be perfect to provide moments of connection and great service. The point is that prolific beats perfect, so just start and just by starting, you will be way ahead of the pack.

Test and Measure

In dentistry we rely on a body of evidence to make clinical decisions. Yet when it comes to making decisions about the business side of dentistry, we seem to rely on anecdotal evidence and "gut instinct". Important though these are, we can actually measure and test the patient experience using more scientific means – the only truth is the result.

I suggest surveying your patients to determine how they felt about their interaction with the practice and critically, whether or not they'd refer family and friends. There are many methods of surveying patients, ranging from simple printed surveys to online systems such as "Survey Monkey". The beauty of an online system is that data is more easily collated and interpreted to identify areas that need improvement in the patient experience.

If we are to continue to surprise and delight our patients, we must strive to constantly improve their experience at our practice. For improvements to have an impact, we must make decisions based on data.

Dealing with Complaints

"It's crucial for companies to realise that the way they handle customer complaints is every bit as important as trying to provide great service in the first place."
Wall Street Journal, 22 September 2008

When a customer makes a complaint they are concerned about two things: the first is that you care about them on a personal level; the second is how you're going to fix their problem so that it doesn't occur again.

There is a natural tendency to become defensive when a complaint is made, particularly if the complaint is unjustified. No one likes to feel criticised. There is a common phrase amongst business people that "the customer is always right." I disagree. The customer is often wrong but that doesn't matter. What matters is the customer's perception of what has happened, and keeping them happy so they continue to frequent your practice.

If the complaint seems unjustified from the perspective of the practice, an ill-considered or intemperate remark by a staff member can see tensions rise and result in an argument and once you're having an argument with a customer, there are no winners. The customer still feels aggrieved and the practice loses a patient. There is a saying that a happy patient might tell two or three people about your practice but an unhappy one will tell the world. So by arguing with one customer, you could lose many more.

One of my early mentors had a saying when it came to handling complaints. He told me *"you can be right or you can be rich. But you can't always be both."*

It makes sense to have a system in place for handling complaints. For all the time and effort many businesses put into improving their customer service, very few have an effective way of handling complaints. The sad truth is that all the work that has gone into trying to give customers a great experience can be wasted if you don't know how to handle complaints effectively.

The good news is that a customer's faith can be restored if a complaint is handled well. Indeed, the Wall Street Journal (22 September 2008) [17] noted that as a result of the "recovery paradox", complaints are an opportunity to turn an unhappy customer into a fierce advocate for the practice.

Customers can tolerate poor service more than failed service recovery. So when a customer makes a complaint, it matters a great deal how you respond initially – not just the words you say but the way you say them and the feelings you attach to them. So what is the best way to respond when a complaint is made?

If there is one emotion that helps diffuse a complaint quickly, it is empathy. So if a complaint is made, our receptionist will respond with *"Oh, that must be frustrating for you"*. But it has to be said in a tone that conveys genuine empathy and concern for the patient. By simply acknowledging the patient's right to feel aggrieved, the tension is immediately taken out of the situation and a solution can be found. Another great way to diffuse a potential complaint is to thank the patient for bringing things to your attention.

Lessons From an Insurance Company

In 2008, a large storm-cell hit the city of Brisbane. Many houses were badly damaged, including ours. The real problem was that we did not yet fully own the house. We had signed a contract to purchase the house, but settlement had not yet taken place. As you can imagine, there were some insurance difficulties to sort out.

The house was insured with a large, well-known insurer. At a time when we were feeling anxious and stressed about the house, the insurance company ignored our calls, appointed new case-managers each time we rang and avoided us as much as they could. It felt like a deliberate attempt to discourage us from pursuing the claim. Rather than trying to help, the company dealt in obfuscation.

Thankfully, we have a very good family solicitor and after five months (and a threat to go on national television), the insurance company accepted liability for the claim and paid for the damage. The fact that it took five months and some legal posturing to get there was ridiculous.

We had been loyal customers of the insurance company until that point. We had multiple policies and paid thousands of dollars annually in terms of insurance premiums. Their handling of our claim and subsequent complaints has ensured that we will never insure with them again.

One of my main frustrations was that the communication from the company was non-existent and that the case-manager kept changing so that there was never any one person familiar with our claim. As each new case-manager tried to come to terms with our claim, it was invariably referred to the legal department for consideration. By the time we called back, the case manager had been replaced and the cycle was repeated. It really felt as though the company didn't care and just wanted us to go away. If there was a textbook way of how to handle a complaint poorly, then they surely wrote it.

Effective Complaint Handling

Handling complaints is everyone's job. When a complaint occurs it is important that the person who first heard the complaint sees the process through to the very end. It doesn't mean other staff cannot be involved in the resolution process but that the initial person co-ordinates the response and communicates with the patient to keep them informed of progress. Patients will then feel their complaint has been taken seriously, a remedy has been found and steps have been put in place to minimise the chance of it occurring again.

It doesn't matter who is wrong and who is right. If you have an unhappy patient, it is their perception that matters. Recovery is powerful and it's in your best interest to find a resolution. If you can validate the patient's feelings, find a way to resolve the problem by saying "yes" (does it really matter if you give a little ground?), and put in place steps to ensure it doesn't happen again; then you've got a really good chance of that patient becoming a loyal advocate of your practice.

Telephone Skills

The telephone is the way that most patients directly experience your practice for the first time. It is therefore critical that their experience on the telephone is of the highest order.

Like all the other tasks that need to be completed in a dental practice, success is related to *how* the task is completed.

After all, there are *ways* and **ways** of going about a task.

The difference in outcome is determined by whether a staff member is on task or on purpose.

When a task is being completed just for the sake of completing it, it will be performed in an entirely different manner from when the staff-member is operating from their "why" or being on-purpose.

For instance, because our "why" is to create a group of friends as our patient-base, our purpose as we go about completing tasks, is to create a group of happy patients who pay their bills, stay at the practice and refer their family and friends.

When staff operate from this perspective, results are far superior than when they simply complete the task without considering the overarching purpose of all activities.

Perhaps one of the most frequent activities in a dental practice is to answer the telephone and make outbound calls. It is critical that staff see these calls as golden opportunities to either add value to existing patients or to welcome new patients to the practice. This comes from being "on purpose" or operating from your "why".

Telephone Basics

Below is a list of the five principles of successful telephone techniques. These principles are deceptively simple and in the daily busyness of practice life, are often overlooked.

However, any practice that aspires to offer exemplary service needs to fully understand the value of a phone call and master these techniques.

1. Smile. Yes, this is possibly the oldest tip in the book and that's because it works.

   By smiling, the receptionist's voice takes on a warmer tone, which is picked up by the caller, helping them to feel more at ease, and making the interaction more enjoyable.

2. Be present. It is important that you're really listening and the caller has your full attention. So, no multitasking please! For a caller there is nothing more annoying than feeling that the other person is distracted and that they have not got your full attention.

   Briefly pausing before you answer the telephone or make a call, is a simple technique that allows you to focus your attention and be present for the call.

3. Use the caller's name. Most people will introduce themselves on the telephone but some will not. In those cases it is important to personalise the call.

   Our receptionist will typically answer the phone by saying: *"Thank you for calling Bespoke Dental. This is Charlie, how may I help you?"* If the caller launches into a conversation without introducing themselves, she will then say, *"Thank you, my name is Charlie and yours is...?"*

   Once the caller offers their name, she is then better positioned to be able to offer the personalised service we strive to provide.

4. Take notes. This might sound contrary to point two, but if a patient is ringing with a toothache, the receptionist will need to be able to convey all the pertinent information to the dentist. We use a "Telephone Information Card" as well as "New Patient Relationship Forms" for this purpose.

5. Empathise and problem solve. We all like to feel understood and that other people care about us. Offer understanding and try to accommodate patient requests where possible.

Dealing with Shoppers

Dealing with shoppers is one of the most overlooked opportunities in a dental practice. When a patient rings asking for a price on a particular item, many of us assume (and I have made this mistake too), that the patient is simply looking for the cheapest price they can find. However what is often overlooked is the fact that such enquiries represent a clear buying signal. It also shows us that the patient has no method of comparison other than price. Herein lies the opportunity.

As always, it is important to stay on-purpose for these types of enquiries and our objective is to move the discussion from price to value and make a booking for the patient.

Caller: Hello, how much does a crown cost?

Us: Thanks again for calling. My name is Charlie and yours is...?

Caller: Bob.

Us: Well Bob, that's a great question. It is impossible to give you an exact figure because the fee will vary with the complexity of your treatment and the type of material that is used. However, using past patients as a guide, I can say the fee would be between $1200 and $1800 depending on your circumstances. How does that compare to the prices you have already?

Bob: Well, I have been quoted $1500 from another practice.

Us: Well Bob, what we do for all of our other patients and then what I'd suggest we do for you is to schedule an examination with Dr Green. He'll perform a thorough examination and go over all of the treatment options available to you as well, outline their pros and cons and then give you an exact fee, rather than a ball park estimate. How does that sound?

Once the patient has booked in for the examination, the decision as to whether to proceed or not, becomes based on far more than price alone – how the patient feels about the level of care they will receive, the patient's perception of the dentist's expertise and so on. The aim is to move the decision-making criteria away from price alone so as to encompass other aspects of care at which we know we excel.

Dealing with Preferred Provider Enquiries

The key to these types of enquiries is to stay on purpose and skilfully move the conversation to one that engenders the development of a relationship.

Caller: Are you a preferred provider with "XYZ" company?

Us: Thanks again for calling. My name is Charlie and yours is...?

Caller: Bob.

Us: Bob, that's a great question. I just missed which company you said you're with?

Bob: "XYZ" Company

Us: Bob, we have many patients at our practice who have their insurance with "XYZ" company, even though we don't participate in that particular scheme. Would you be interested to know why those patients come here?

Bob: Sure.

Us: Well, what they tell us is that they appreciate the quality of care and level of personalised service that they receive here. And that's why they prefer to come to our practice. What we do for those patients and what we'd be happy to do for you as well is to help you process your claim so you can get the maximum rebate from your insurance company. How does that sound to you?

Bob: That sounds great.

Our aim in this conversation is to let Bob know that we treat many patients who have their insurance with "XYZ" Company and that they love the service they receive, even though we're not preferred providers for that company. By demonstrating this social proof, Bob is encouraged to visit our practice so that he can experience the same excellent level of care experienced by other patients who have their insurance with "XYZ" Company.

Finding a Suitable Appointment Time

Once the caller has agreed to an appointment the next step is to find a time that is mutually convenient. I have literally seen one particular receptionist offer an appointment for Monday at 8am. When the patient declined that appointment, they were offered 9am, 10 am and even 11am. In the end, the patient left without an appointment but with the feeling that the practice was desperate. As anyone on the dating scene knows, there is nothing less attractive than being too available.

No matter how busy (or not) the dentist may be, I recommend a cascading series of alternate choice questions to find a suitable appointment-time. This allows the patient to feel like they are "choosing" their appointment-time while the practice maintains the integrity of their appointment book.

Us: Bob, when it comes to making an appointment, which days of the week work best for you?

Bob: Monday and Wednesday are my best days.

Us: And do you prefer a morning or afternoon appointment?

Bob: Mornings usually work best for me.

Us: OK that's great. I have Monday the 3rd of February at 8am or Wednesday the 5th of February at 10am available. Which one of those works best for you Bob?

Bob: Monday the 3rd February at 8am works best for me. I can come and see you before I go to work.

Us: That's great Bob. I have you booked in to see Dr Green at 8am on Monday the 3rd of February.

Using the Phone Call to Generate Patient Flow

A key metric we track in our practice is the ratio of incoming calls to appointments booked. We are looking to measure the efficiency of the reception staff at generating additional patients from the phone call.

The technique is very simple and highly effective. When a patient phones to make an appointment, the receptionist will book that appointment and seek commitment in the usual manner. (See Chapter 6 – Eliminating Cancellations for how to obtain appointment commitment.) Once that's been completed, she follows up simply by saying; *"Bob, we're looking forward to seeing you at 8am on Monday 3rd February. Now, while I have you on the phone, is there anyone else in the family who needs an appointment?"*

Over time, this simple follow up question has significantly improved patient flow and added well over one hundred thousand dollars in revenue.

The most successful practices I come across see a phone call as an opportunity to deliver real value to existing patients as well as potential new patients. Mastering these skills represents an opportunity to set your practice apart from others, creating a compelling reason for patients to frequent your practice rather than another one.

A Note to Specialists

To continually grow your practice as a specialist, you need to be looking at ways to provide a great customer experience for both customers – the patient and referring practitioner.

Depending on your practice, referring dentists are often the best source of qualified, pre-sold patients. Because dentists often do the hard work of convincing the patient of the need for treatment and then endorsing you, these patients are far more likely to accept treatment. Clearly it is in your interest to nurture a relationship with your referring dentist and ensure that they too have an excellent experience when they interact with your practice.

I have outlined the principles of providing a great customer experience. These principles are as applicable to a referring dentist as they are for patients: you will need to determine the service standards you'd like to be known for; map out the touch-points a dentist will have with your practice; and then choreograph the ideal experience that they will have with your practice. Another great way to determine how to "Wow" your referrers is to determine the major problems they experience in their practice and see if there is a way that you can help overcome these.

One of the simplest ways for a specialist to provide a great experience for their referring dentist is to provide an exceptional and seamless experience for the patient. As general dentists, we look to retain our patients for life. So one of the most helpful things a specialist can do is to assist in that process. It is helpful if the specialist can take the time to reinforce the patients' trust in the referring dentist with an edifying comment about them.

There are many other ways you can "Wow" your referring dentists. You're only limited by your imagination. A friend of mine who is an endodontist is fond of the saying *"one hand washes the other."* Where possible, he tries to return the patient to the general practice pre-sold on the next phase of the treatment plan. He will even offer to place a core in the tooth following endodontic treatment. So if a crown is indicated, the dentist can book that straight in without needing to take time to place a core. For those who wish it, he also uses his microscope to prepare margins that would be difficult to prepare otherwise.

Other specialists whom I know look to provide value to their referrers by hosting "Professional Development" (CPD) events.

You will notice that all of the examples that I have provided show the specialist helping the referring dentist solve a problem of some sort, whether it be completing difficult treatment to a high standard, helping solve a busyness issue or making CPD accessible and inexpensive – they solve problems.

As a specialist, one of the best ways to retain a solid group of referrers is to understand what keeps them awake at night and look to offer solutions to those problems through the delivery of specialist dental care.

Action Steps

1. Map each interaction your patients have with the practice (touch-points) to determine the patient journey. These should include interactions the patient can have with your practice before they arrive, during their appointment, after their appointment and between appointments.

2. Modify the list of service standards to suit your own practice. Aim to create a series of moments of connection throughout the patient journey.

3. Examine how well you apply each of the service standards at each touch-point in the practice. Look at ways to do more. Be creative and dare to be different!

4. Ensure your receptionist knows who is due to come through the door at any given time and is ready to greet them by name. The morning meeting is a great opportunity to choreograph this.

5. Ensure all staff are present – mentally and emotionally – for your patients. Understand that your patients are looking to be cared for not worked on.

6. Role play scenarios in a staff meeting where you cannot say no to a patient request, even when it is not something you initially want to do. Find creative ways to say "yes" to the patient without violating the needs of the practice.

7. Brainstorm with your practice staff what you can do to make your patients' day that little bit better or their experience with you that bit more enjoyable.

8. Brainstorm how can you introduce an element of fun into your practice. What interests do you or your staff have that might translate into interest or fun from the patients' perspectives?

9. Create a survey aimed at discovering how patients feel about their experience at your practice. Collate the results to see what common themes or trends emerge. This data will allow you to make more intelligent decisions about how well customer service is being delivered at each touch-point in the practice and what improvements can be made.

10. Establish a protocol for handling complaints. Where possible, empower staff to see a complaint through until it is rectified.

11. Implement skills training for answering the telephone.

Download the Workbook

Remember to download the companion workbook to access checklists, cheat sheets and other resources. It is available at:
www.drjessegreen.com/retention/workbook

6

WOULD YOU STAND ME UP?

Life moves pretty fast.
If you don't stop and
look around once in a while,
you could miss it.

—

Ferris Bueller - 1986

WOULD YOU STAND ME UP?

Cancellations and no-shows represent a major loss of productivity in a dental practice. Furthermore, they adversely affect our ability to provide patients with the treatment that they need to maintain their dental health. Moreover, cancellations and no shows are often the precursor to the ultimate loss of a patient from the practice.

Clearly, eliminating cancellations and no shows from your practice would have a positive effect on patient retention, the profitability and stability of earnings of the practice as well as the delivery of patient care.

Many years ago, a mentor taught me that the reason for an appointment was to book another appointment. In other words, our patients always leave with an appointment or at the very least, an agreed-upon way for us to initiate contact with them.

It struck me then as it still does now, that this single concept has the power to transform a practice from mediocre to great, by ensuring the retention of patients.

Why Do People Cancel or Not Show Up?

There are many reasons patients give when trying to cancel or failing to attend their appointments. Some of the reasons are perfectly legitimate – sickness, family emergency and so on. I accept that these events happen from time-to-time. By and large however, most cancellations and no-shows are not the result of an unexpected, calamitous event. There are three main circumstances that contribute to cancellations, however the common thread is that the appointment is not perceived as being valuable enough to remain the patient's top priority and most no-shows occur simply because of that fact: the appointment was not the patient's number one priority at that time.

Secondly, if a patient has cancelled or not shown up in the past without a consequence, the practice has, in effect, given its tacit approval for this behaviour. The lack of consequences for no-shows and cancellations sends a powerful message to patients that such behaviour is acceptable.

The third reason that patients don't attend their appointments is because they have not been asked to commit to the appointed time. When a commitment is first sought by the practice and then given by the patient, the likelihood of a last minute cancellation or no-show is greatly reduced.

Eliminating Cancellations and No Shows

Because most cancellations occur as a result of competing priorities, it is important that the practice takes the time to communicate the value patients are receiving when making appointments. As we discussed in Chapter 4, value should be built and communicated to the patient before, during and after the appointment.

In this instance, we use language to link the patient's attendance to their emotional motivators and concerns or "hot buttons". In essence, we're showing how attending the appointment will meet an emotional need of the patient thereby ensuring it remains a priority in their life. When dental treatment is perceived as being of as high a priority as their emotional needs, patients will typically find a way to attend their appointments.

In Chapter 4, I mentioned I'd had a conversation with some women about the attachment they felt to their hairdressers. I learned that these particular women would do almost anything to avoid having to reschedule a hairdressing appointment. During our conversation they mentioned to me that there were several reasons for this. The primary reason was that they'd have to wait a long time for another appointment due to the busyness of the salon. The women expressed concerns about not looking and feeling their best, whether it be as a result of a hairstyle getting too long, or from the re-growth of dyed hair. Because the hairdressing appointment met the emotional motivators and concerns of the women at a certain level, they placed a high value on the appointment and the consequences of missing it were too much to bear.

Interestingly, some of the women in the group also said they felt that by not keeping their appointment they'd be letting their hairdresser down. These women had a strong connection with their hairdresser and as a result of their relationship, felt a sense of responsibility and obligation to the salon to attend.

As I mentioned in the introduction of this book, the importance of forming personal connections with patients is a recurring theme because they are so critical to the delivery of dental care, including the prevention of cancellations and no-shows. When the relationship between the patient and the dentist transcends the transactional level and moves to a more personal relationship, patients feel an obligation to the practice just as the practice feels an obligation to them. Furthermore, patients begin to care about the well-being of you and your practice in a way that they would not have done previously.

For the women I spoke to, the combined effect of valuing the appointment, having a relationship with the hairdresser and an understanding of the consequences of missing the appointment, meant that they would rearrange just about anything to ensure that they could attend their hairdressing appointment.

In his book, Influence – The Psychology of Persuasion, Robert Cialdini discusses six psychological principles that are involved in the ability to be influential. One of these is the principle of Commitment and Consistency. Cialdini states, *"Once we have made a choice or taken a stand, we will encounter personal and interpersonal pressures to behave consistently with that commitment."*(P57)[18]

The premise of Cialdini's argument is that when a declaration is made publicly, it is far more difficult to resile from. He also makes the point that the more effort it takes to make that declaration, the more internal pressure there is to behave in a manner that is consistent with the commitment. We know this to be true from our own experience.

At the beginning of 2014, I set a goal to run a half-marathon. So that I could invoke the principle of commitment and consistency on myself, I announced my intention to run the Canberra half-marathon on social media, and also sought to raise money for charity by encouraging family and friends to sponsor me. There were plenty of times I didn't want to train and if I hadn't committed so publicly, I might well have been tempted to pull out. By invoking commitment and consistency within myself, I achieved that goal.

The same holds true for dental appointments. We need to seek a commitment from the patient that they will attend. If we can extract that commitment, then the law of commitment and consistency will be invoked and the likelihood of the patient cancelling is considerably diminished.

How is this accomplished in a practical sense? There are several ways to invoke the law of commitment and consistency and the first is to have the receptionist simply ask for the commitment once the appointment has been made and accepted. For instance, our receptionist says something like *"Mrs. Jones, we have you booked in to see Dr Green at 2pm next Wednesday. Will you be here?"* She says it with a smile and in a light tone that is inquisitive rather than confrontational. The patient invariably replies "yes" because they have just negotiated an appointment that suits them. By making the public declaration to come to the appointment they agreed to in the first place, the law of Commitment and Consistency has been invoked and the likelihood of the patient cancelling is significantly reduced.

What to Do If a Patient Cancels

As much as we aim to prevent cancellations and no-shows, we don't yet live in a utopian world and last minute cancellations can occasionally occur. So when they do happen we need to know how to handle them so that they don't happen repeatedly.

The most common "offender" in any practice is a patient who is new to the practice: the reason is that there is not yet an established relationship between the patient and the practice.

In the event of a cancellation or no-show, it is important to avoid resorting to quoting the practice policy. When the practice recites some draconian policy chapter and verse, the opportunity to educate the patient about the impact that the cancellation has on the practice and the patient themselves is lost. Not only that, the "It's our policy" conversation can come across as being patronising and condescending. If the patient is made to feel like a naughty child, they can easily take offence and leave the practice altogether.

A cancellation is an opportunity to revisit what motivates the patient from an emotional perspective. By that, I mean the motivators and concerns or "hot buttons" a patient has around their dental treatment. If the dentist has spent time developing a relationship with the patient during the examination process, then these should be recorded on the patient's file.

When the phone call comes, the receptionist should open the patient's file and look for the patient's "hot buttons" as well as checking for a past history of broken appointments. The "hot buttons" are used to gently remind the patient why they wanted to have treatment in the first instance and see if they can be persuaded to keep the appointment.

"Mrs. Jones, I see from your file that you've had some pain on the upper left-hand side. In order to avoid another episode like that Dr Green really needs to attend to the cavities on the right hand side. Is there any way you can make today's appointment?" It is important to then pause.

The purpose of the pause is to create a little bit of dramatic tension. Pauses can be uncomfortable. You will know yourself that when there is a pause in conversation there is a natural tendency to fill the void. The first person to speak is usually the one to acquiesce.

This is not some smooth sales technique or manipulation. The purpose of motivating the patient to keep the appointment they agreed to, is to ensure that they receive the best possible dental care and that the practice is not left with a hole in its production.

If the patient really cannot keep the appointment, then it is important a new one is made and the patient is asked to commit to the new time. As a general rule, I like to play a little "hard to get" and not be too available for the new appointment.

As we all remember from our days of dating, being too available is not necessarily an attractive quality. If you let the patient feel you're at their complete disposal, you can be treated as a convenience rather than a trusted advisor. Obviously, each practice must meet its own scheduling needs but I like to ensure that if a patient cancels, they wait at least a week before coming in – even if there is time available the next day. For me, it is about educating the patient in that cancelling at short notice comes with consequences.

However it is really important not to become too punitive in this approach. The receptionist needs to be emotionally intelligent enough to determine which cancellations are genuine emergencies as opposed to those that occur because the patient didn't prioritise their dental care. If in doubt, my default position is to remember our purpose – to create a practice of happy patients who pay, stay and refer. So, I look to accommodate them, but if they cancel a second time, I certainly make them wait.

If the patient is not in a position to make a new appointment, then a time should be agreed upon for the practice to contact them with a view to booking a new one.

On the odd occasion I have a recalcitrant patient who doesn't respect our time, I have a conversation around our philosophy – not our policy.

"Mr. Smith, when you first came to our practice, I indicated that our philosophy is to be as comprehensive in our approach to dental treatment as possible. When you keep cancelling your appointment at short notice, I am not able to provide the level of care our patients have come to enjoy and expect. I really need you to attend the appointments that you schedule with our practice. Can you help me with that?"

On nearly every occasion the patient will agree and attend their appointments thereafter. If I have a patient who cancels or misses the appointments again (first checking the legitimacy of the reason), I am then in the position of asking them to seek treatment elsewhere. This might sound a little harsh but if a patient repeatedly refuses to prioritise their treatment and does not respect our time, then I am not the person to best treat them.

It is important that the practice nips in the bud cancellations and no-shows. As I mentioned earlier, by not taking action you are implicitly training patients to believe that cancellations are acceptable.

Power of Language

There is little doubt about the power of language. Words have the ability to excite, inspire, spark action, soothe and comfort. However, they also have the ability to cause offence, create mistrust and destroy confidence.

Language first informs our thoughts, then actions, and ultimately our habits. It is our habits that create the results, both positive and negative, in our lives. Despite this power, many people give little thought as to how we use language in our daily lives and the profound effect it can have on others.

Because language carries such meaning and power, it's important we use words with specific intent. If we use them carelessly or without thought, we can inadvertently confer a meaning or significance that is neither appropriate nor desirable.

For this reason we strive to use language that reinforces positive outcomes. Parents of young children will see this principle in action every day. A friend of mine tells the story of her young daughter who enjoyed playing with the sliding door. My friend, aware of her language, would say, "Remember to keep your fingers safe," which her daughter did. When a relative came to visit, he too was concerned for her safety. However, his language was more negative and he said, "Don't do that. You'll slam your fingers in the door." And for the first time, she did just that. Even with the same intent, different words produce different outcomes, hence we need to choose them carefully.

In terms of patient flow, we prefer to use the phrase "change of schedule" instead of the word "cancellation" in our practice. I have long believed that by removing this word from our vocabulary it conveys the message that we just don't get cancellations.

Equally, when patients request an earlier appointment than is currently available, we place them on a "priority list" rather than a cancellation list. The term "priority list" leaves the patient feeling important without implying that cancellations are part of our daily practice routine.

Some may think that we're dealing in semantics here but I have had many patients over the years comment about how they had tried to get an earlier appointment but could not because "You guys just don't get cancellations." I can tell you that the patients who made those comments to me never cancelled or failed to attend their appointment.

Another simple example of the use of positive language is seen when establishing a date for recall examinations. We have learned to replace the phrase "six month recall" with an indication of exactly when we'd like them to return for their recall examination. A client of mine has taken it a step further by preferring to use the term "preventive maintenance appointment" instead of recall examination. So in this instance, the patient would be invited to return for their preventive maintenance appointment in March (or whatever month represents a six month time period). By using positive and specific language, we are creating a positive connotation for the appointment and setting an expectation of their return visit.

We work hard to reduce the impact of cancellations and no-shows and I'm mindful about the message we communicate directly or indirectly to our patients. Being aware of the power of language and consciously choosing the type of language we use has had an enormously positive impact on patient flow and patient retention in our practice.

Setting and Respecting Boundaries

Building a practice that is patient-centric doesn't mean we have to cater to patients' every whim or be treated purely as a convenience. The relationship between the practice and the patient must be a two-way street, based on mutual respect and obligations.

However, like all relationships, there will be boundaries that need to be set and respected. Dental practices will have all sorts of boundaries – verbal and non-verbal – around areas such as failing to attend appointments, cancellations and the payment of accounts. The problem for many dental practices is that they don't articulate their boundaries, so that when those boundaries are violated, the practitioner may end up feeling upset while the patient remains oblivious to the situation.

If boundaries haven't been set in the past, then when a violation occurs it really boils down to having a conversation with the patient about them. This conversation is best had from the point-of-view of a philosophy and how these boundaries improve patient care rather than from the point-of-view of a practice policy. Although the difference is subtle, the end result of each conversation is vastly different. When you approach the conversation with a genuine concern for delivering optimal care, patients will typically respond more favourably than if they feel scolded for not adhering to a practice policy.

Conversations in which boundaries are communicated to patients require a degree of skill, sensitivity and emotional intelligence. It is important that whoever has these conversations possesses these attributes. Many times dentists will delegate this role to the receptionist or practice manager. On occasion they may be the most appropriate person to have the conversation but more often, the task is delegated because the dentist is afraid of a potential confrontation. The first point I'd make is that when the conversation is had from a philosophical, rather than a policy standpoint, the risk of confrontation is significantly reduced. The second point I'd make is that delegating uncomfortable tasks is not management but a lack of leadership.

Once boundaries have been set, consistency is necessary for patients. If you flip-flop, you will appear indecisive and the whole process has been undone.

One of the most common boundaries that needs to be communicated is the need for payment. While electronic payment methods have reduced the overall level of bad debts, it can sometimes be the case that payments are not made in a timely fashion. We experienced this situation when we purchased our first practice, for the previous owner had run an "accounts" system. After we took over, there was an expectation that accounts would continue to be issued and subsequently, payments were slow to arrive. These arrangements meant our cash-flow was lumpy and we needed to move to a system where patients paid on the day of treatment.

In the first instance, our boundaries were communicated in general terms by outlining fresh payment terms in literature, such as a practice brochure or "new patient" letter. In this way, patients new to the practice were unaware of the previous payment system.

We also communicated our boundaries with a waiting room sign. However, rather than an abrupt "payment is required on the day of treatment" kind of sign, it said "Thank you for helping us continue to provide the highest level of care by paying your account on the day of treatment". As you can see, the underlying message is the same but by using positive language to thank the patients and by explaining a little of our philosophy, the message was more subtle, and certainly pointed to a gentler approach.

Most patients moved across to the new system without any fuss. However there were two patients reluctant to switch. In the end, I had a conversation with them to try and understand their concerns. Both patients were gainfully employed and were not in any particular financial stress. It seemed they wanted to manage their own cash-flow by deferring payments for as long as possible. After explaining our position in an amicable fashion, I asked if they would be comfortable with the new arrangements. One patient was and remained loyal to the practice while the other patient indicated he would not make the transition to the new system. Consequently, I explained that we were not a good fit for one another and had the unenviable task of asking him to seek treatment elsewhere. We made every aspect of the transfer as easy as possible and parted company on good terms.

Are there ever exceptions? Are there times we consciously choose to relax our boundaries? Yes there are. For instance, when a patient embarks on a substantial treatment plan and doesn't have the whole amount up front, we do allow them, on some occasions, to pay it off. Here's the point though. Boundaries are still set and respected. Under these circumstances, the practice and the patient negotiate mutually acceptable terms and communicate these boundaries by having a signed financial agreement in place. The idea in this instance, is to structure an agreement that allows the patient to have the treatment they need and remain at our practice which maintains the financial well-being of the practice.

The terms surrounding payment of fees is just one example of setting boundaries. There are of course, many other situations where this can and should occur in a practice. It has been my experience and the experience of many other dentists that once boundaries are set, communicated and adhered to, practice life becomes much easier for all parties.

Consequences

There will be some patients who despite a conversation around boundaries, will continue to test them. For example, last minute cancellations have a direct impact on my ability to provide ideal care, not only for that particular patient but also for other patients who could have used that appointment time.

There have been times when despite my best efforts to communicate my boundaries regarding these cancellations, the behaviour still persisted. I came to realise that unless there was a consequence for these patients, there was no way they'd respect my boundaries in the future. Everyone will determine what works best for their own practice but in my practice, we make a patient wait a few weeks before we're available to see them again. Some practices that I know of have asked "offending" patients to prepay a non-refundable deposit before the next appointment is made. Other practices choose to impose a cancellation fee for missed appointments. I prefer not to use the latter method because to me, it's punitive and can inadvertently communicate the message that cancellations are acceptable if the fine is paid. I prefer to encourage the patient to attend through positive reinforcement and other positive and appropriate means.

As I have previously discussed, at our practice I prefer to initially motivate the patients to keep the appointment. However, if cancellations persist, I prefer that patient to move on, enabling me to dedicate my time and energy to the patients who are loyal and who do keep their appointments.

Of course, there is no right or wrong in these circumstances and what works for one practice may not work for another. What's important is to know how you'll handle such situations before they arise.

But I Need Patients

When the discussion of no-shows and cancellations turns to consequences, some dentists break out in a sweat. "But I need patients. I can't afford to lose them!" is a typical comment that I hear because they're worried about patient flow in competitive times.

My response is simple: you don't want patients who don't respect your time. You're better off focusing on other marketing initiatives and tightening systems in order to really look after and retain your existing A-grade patients and thereby attracting more of them.

As dentists, we often try to be all things to all people. However as I discussed in Chapter 3, the aim isn't to do business with everyone, but rather to attract and retain ideal patients – those who believe what we believe. By setting and maintaining boundaries we can create a core group of patients who buy into why we do what we do and value us as trusted advisors. Failure to set boundaries or to have consequences for missed appointments results in a lack of structure, sporadic patient flow, diminished profitability and reduced professional satisfaction.

Action Steps

1. Review the ways you build and communicate value for your patients' next appointments.

2. Write a script to handle possible cancellations and practise them with your team.

3. Examine commonly used negative-sounding expressions in your practice and look at how they can be transformed into positive expressions.

4. Understand where you will set boundaries in your practice.

5. If a patient does cancel, what consequences will stem from that decision? Map this out for your practice.

Download the Workbook

Remember to download the companion workbook to access checklists, cheat sheets and other resources. It is available at:

www.drjessegreen.com/retention/workbook

7

DON'T LEAVE ME THIS WAY

Maverick:
She's lost that loving feeling.

Goose:
I hate it when she does that.

—

Top Gun, 1986

DON'T LEAVE ME THIS WAY

Every practice has patients who leave for one reason or another and most of the time we don't see it coming. It is only when we receive a request to transfer records that we realise a patient has not been happy at our practice.

Most dentists have an unconscious yet predictable response when a patient leaves. Sometimes this response serves us and at other times it does not.

In the past, my response to a patient leaving was to take it very personally. I went through a whole array of emotions: at first I felt rejected, thinking about what we must have done to make them want to leave; then I wondered what the other practice offered that we didn't and finally, I went through a rather churlish phase of thinking "Well stuff you too! Good riddance!"

The problem with riding the emotional roller-coaster is that we can get so caught up in our own feelings that we can forget to take the opportunity to learn from the experience.

After talking to hundreds of dentists over the years, I learned that I wasn't alone. It seems most dentists love to be loved by their patients, so much so that a patient leaving evokes a strong emotional response.

If we want to take control of our businesses, we need to get past the hurt and try to develop an understanding of why the patient decided to leave. Once we know that, we can prevent more patients leaving and ensure those who do leave, do so on the best possible terms rather than leaving with bad feelings.

Why Do Patients Leave?

There are a multitude of reasons a patient may leave the practice, ranging from poor service, dissatisfaction over fees, or a lack of confidence in the dentist's ability to perform the prescribed treatment. However for all the reasons a patient may give, it is my experience that all of these reasons can be grouped into three main categories: lack of a relationship with, and loyalty to, the practice; a lack of perceived value; or a negative experience leading to a breach of trust.

1. Lack of a Relationship With and Loyalty To the Practice

Human beings are social creatures by nature and in general, like to form relationships with people they interact with. I have already mentioned that relationships are the glue that holds society together, or in our case – a practice together. Relationships create a sense of loyalty and mutual obligation.

In the absence of a relationship, patients feel no loyalty to the practice, making them an easier target for other practices with slick marketing.

What's more, the lack of a relationship means there is an insufficient balance in the "emotional bank account" to cover a potential withdrawal if the patient were to have a negative experience at the practice. In those circumstances, the patient is more likely to leave than if there had been a relationship to fall back on.

2. Lack of Perceived Value

If patients are not educated about the distinction between value and price, there is a risk that your services can be commoditised. Once services are commoditised the primary method of comparison becomes price.

A dental practice is an inherently expensive business to operate. We all recognise that the cost of attending a dentist can be high. However, we need to take responsibility for impressing upon our patients both the importance of their dental care and educating them about the value that our treatment offers.

There will always be someone willing to provide dental services more cheaply and if they have no reason to be loyal to your practice, patients can easily be lured away by the prospect of saving a few dollars in the short-term.

When quality dental care is not a priority in a patient's life it is easy for them to disappear into the deep blue yonder, never to be seen again whilst we wonder what happened. So be sure to build value for what you do.

3. A Negative Experience Leading to a Breach of Trust

A negative experience typically relates to a violation of one of the three factors affecting trust that I discussed in Chapter 4: ability (a clinical failure), behaviour (a poor customer service experience) or character (perceived dishonesty or lack of integrity).

I have already discussed the fact that clinical competence is crucial to building a sustainable practice. However, we all accept that from time-to-time clinical outcomes are not all what we'd hope for. Sometimes this leads to our own disappointment as well as the disappointment of the patient. Clinical failures can quickly undermine the confidence a patient may have in a practitioner's ability to perform treatment. Left unresolved, the patient will seek treatment from a practitioner in whom they have confidence.

A negative experience may also take the form of a poor service experience for the patient. While the clinical dentistry may well have been performed to a high standard, if the behaviour of the staff within the practice leads to an impression of indifference, a lack of empathy, or even rudeness, then the patient may feel sufficiently aggrieved to leave the practice.

The other factor that can lead patients to feel as though their trust has been breached, relates to whether or not the dentist is perceived to be acting ethically. By and large, dentists are a very ethical group of people. Like every group however, there will always be some who operate entirely for their own benefit. It is entirely possible to operate a practice that provides a genuine win-win-win. A win for the health and well-being of the patient, a win for the performance of the practice and, a win for the dentist. Building a practice that is successful over many years necessitates that dentists operate from a win-win-win perspective at all times.

Therefore, it is critical that if a patient does have a negative experience, it is dealt with swiftly, fairly, and with empathy. A lack of resolution of a grievance or a perceived lack of caring is a very swift way to lose a patient.

What To Do When a Patient Leaves

The way we find out why patients leave is to conduct an exit interview. These work for several reasons and more often than not, vexed patients just want to be heard and have their feelings about the practice acknowledged. Exit interviews also work for the practice owner because we get to hear feedback of which we would otherwise have been ignorant.

If we can genuinely listen to the patient and take the criticism on board, this is a golden opportunity to improve service delivery and perception in the marketplace

I have a particular sequence I like to follow when conducting the exit interview – aimed at getting as many patients as possible to provide feedback – no matter how bad it may be.

Here is my process:

1. When a request for records is received, my practice manager will call to confirm the request. During that conversation she indicates that we're sad to see them go and asks if they'd mind helping us learn from the experience by completing the exit interview.

2. Depending on their preference, the patient is then either sent a link to a survey on SurveyMonkey.com, or is mailed our own questionnaire with a stamped, self addressed return envelope.

3. When the questionnaire is returned, I will call them and thank them for taking the time to provide feedback.

We examine the feedback and look for opportunities for improvement. Interestingly, in our practice and those of my clients, we have found that most patients have left over what turned out to be miscommunications rather than genuinely poor service or treatment. So being able to talk to them is a great way to clear up any misunderstandings.

When I call the patient, my only goal is to thank them for their feedback, let them know we have "heard" them and to try to ensure their final experience with the practice is a positive one. Generally, the patient leaves happy in the knowledge that their "grievance" has been heard. This drastically reduces the chance of the patient making adverse comments about the practice to their family and friends. Sometimes the conversation goes so well that the patient decides to stay.

Unless I really don't want to see the patient again, I close the conversation by letting them know that the door is always open and that we're happy to help them in the future should they wish it. Over the years we have had quite a few patients return and even refer other patients.

No-one likes having patients leave. But if someone decides your practice is not right for them, the best thing you can do is try to make the best of the situation and learn as much as you can in the process.

Action Steps

1. Develop a protocol to deal with patients who indicate they're leaving.

2. Create a questionnaire to use in the exit interview.

3. Once the questionnaire has been received, facilitate the transfer of records as smoothly as possible, ensuring the patients' final interaction with the practice is positive.

4. Be sure to leave the door open for the patient to return.

Download the Workbook

Remember to download the companion workbook to access checklists, cheat sheets and other resources. It is available at:

www.drjessegreen.com/retention/workbook

8

BUILDING
THE TRIBE

We may all have come on
different ships, but we're in
the same boat now.

—

Martin Luther King Jr

BUILDING THE TRIBE

Creating a viable dental practice requires that we focus on creating a core group of patients who continue to frequent the practice, pay their bills and refer others. We call that group of patients our Tribe.

Building a Tribe requires a deliberate focus on improving patient flow using what I call the Three R's of Patient Flow – Retention, Reactivation and Recruitment.

The mistake most dentists make with their marketing is that they tend to focus primarily on patient recruitment. Of the Three R's, Recruitment is the most expensive. The most successful marketing campaigns place equal value on Retention, Reactivation and Recruitment.

As I discussed earlier, patient retention is the foundation of any marketing plan because it provides a platform from which the Tribe can grow. There is little point recruiting new patients if they are not retained. This section deals with the reactivation of those patients who have fallen by the wayside as well as the most effective yet inexpensive form of patient recruitment: word-of-mouth marketing.

Hidden Sources of Patients

Some old, well-established practices that I've worked with over the years have had issues with patient flow despite their longevity. It always seemed a little odd to me that these "premier" practices were struggling to fill their appointment books.

However, when we dug a little below the surface to see what was going on, it wasn't so much that they had a lack of patients, it was more that they were leaking patients much faster than they could attract them. It is not uncommon to see practices focus their efforts on attracting many new patients but neglect the ones they already have. Rather than spending more time, energy and money on marketing for new patients, plugging the leak and concentrating on keeping the patients you have is the number one thing you need to do. Your best patient is the one you already have.

One particular practice had let over ten thousand patients leave over a period of seven years without having a method of recalling them. (Note: that is not a typo – they actually "leaked" over 10,000 patients!). Assuming the average number of patients per full-time dentist is 2,000, they let enough patients for five full-time dentists walk out of the door, with no structured method of remaining in contact with them. Assuming an average new patient value of $500 (which is very conservative), that's $5,000,000 that they just let walk away. That doesn't even take into consideration the lifetime value of those patients, or the additional patients that might have been referred by them. The size of this blunder is monumental. The fact that it took seven years to detect, is unforgivable. If they were a public company, the directors could have been sued for negligence!

What had happened was that the receptionist who had been at the practice for over thirty years was grossly incompetent. When the practice digitised, the recall was not set up properly and the receptionist did not check the systems and was not curious enough to wonder where all the patients were going. She openly discussed that the practice operated on a feast or famine basis. However, because she was paid her wage, irrespective of the practice's performance, she had little incentive (other than professional pride which was clearly lacking) to remedy the situation.

Valuable Lesson for Me

I had first-hand experience with the above practice because I was an employed dentist there at the time. I had been watching my appointment book thin out over time and expressed concerns to the principals of the practice. My concerns seemed to fall on deaf ears.

I would spend a considerable amount of time with patients, discussing treatment options with them and helping them decide the best course of action. I would then escort the patient to the reception and hand the patient over to the receptionist and explain what we had planned and what needed to be done first.

As I left the reception, I was dismayed to hear the receptionist tell the patient that they could call back to make an appointment without first offering to make one for them then and there. The patient was a bit confused and ambled off, feeling a little uncertain about the way forward. Again, there was no mechanism in place to re-establish contact with the patient.

These patients had accepted treatment and were ready to proceed. The receptionist, due to her incompetence, had completely undone all the work I had done in the surgery and in more than a few cases, adversely affected patient care.

At the same time we discovered there had been 10,000 patients leave without a recall being set, we also discovered that there was over $700,000 worth of treatment that had been planned but not booked in.

Clearly there was a problem with reception and the receptionist. The receptionist was slowly but surely killing the business. I decided to take matters into my own hands. I started making appointments in my surgery and bypassing the receptionist for anything other than the payment of the account. While my patient flow was still not where I wanted it to be, I did manage to stem the tide.

Over time, the appointment books of the principals began to thin out as well. They were well aware of the receptionist's shortcomings and had openly discussed the idea of sacking her. However, there were some concerns about that course of action – due to the fact that paying out her accrued entitlements would have a significant impact on the cash-flow of the practice.

As the principals' appointment books began to thin even further I felt sure that they'd have the impetus to act. And act they did! But not in the way I expected. They sacked me and absorbed my patient flow into their books.

That was the first and only time in my life that I have been sacked from a job. At first I felt angry and humiliated. After a while I began to see it for what it was – a lack of leadership and an unwillingness to address the core issue affecting the practice.

There were so many lessons that I learned while working at this practice that I would not have otherwise learned. Hence my initial anger and sense of hurt has long been replaced by a sense of gratitude.

The first lesson is obvious – make sure you have a structured recall system. It is also critical that the practice measures the effectiveness of their recall system. That is, for every hundred recalls sent, how many appointments are made? I was recently working with a practice which is very diligent in sending recalls and yet had patient flow issues in one particular month. When we looked at the numbers in more detail we discovered that the recall system was operating at 47% efficiency. Thankfully, this particular dentist is very proactive and that issue was nipped in the bud immediately.

This paves the way for the second lesson – that prevention is much better than cure. Ensuring patients are recalled properly is a far less demanding task than trying to reactivate them after the fact.

As I have mentioned before, my philosophy is that the purpose of an appointment is to book another appointment. Where possible, I like every patient to leave the practice with their next appointment scheduled. Even if the next appointment is a recall (preventive maintenance) examination due in six months' time, I like to book that immediately. We have a system in place where the patients are reminded of the appointment several weeks ahead of time, so that if there is a diary clash, the appointment can be changed without inconveniencing the practice or the patient. From there, we confirm the appointment in our usual manner. It is much simpler to operate this way than trying to coax patients back to the practice after an extended absence.

The third lesson is to book patients in for treatment as soon as they accept it. Once the appointment is booked (and commitment obtained), the chance of the treatment being completed as per the treatment plan is very high. If patients leave without booking an appointment, set an agreed time for you to re-establish contact with the aim of scheduling an appointment for them.

Reactivation

Typically, when there is an issue with patient flow, the first response of the practice is to call someone like me and ask for some assistance with their marketing. Oftentimes, the practice is looking for the silver bullet that will cure their patient flow issues in a short time.

One of the key messages I try to impart to dentists is that building a sustainable, successful dental practice is a medium to long-term project. Sure we can create short-term sales surges but that's what they are. It is much better to move beyond that to the point of having a constant stream of high quality patients who know you, like you, pay their bills, stay at the practice, and refer others.

Allow me to let you in on a secret that most marketers don't want you to know: there is more money wasted on marketing than it actually delivers in terms of new business. That probably sounds odd coming from someone who helps dentists and specialists grow their practices. Here's what I mean: It is easy to be seduced by the latest fad in marketing. Sure, there is a place for social media, email marketing, public relations and other forms of external marketing. However, you get a much better return on internal marketing because your existing patients already have a relationship with you and you can gain access to them quickly and inexpensively.

So, before undertaking any glitzy marketing campaign, my advice is to carefully examine your existing patient base and look for opportunities to market to them directly.

Most practice management computer systems have the ability to generate a large number of reports. Some reports you'll want to view, others not so much. The ones you need at this point are those that tell you which patients are overdue for their recall (preventive maintenance) examination, as well as identifying those patients who have outstanding treatment.

Once these lists have been prepared, it is important to encourage patients to return to the practice by conducting a reactivation campaign.

Reactivation campaigns are especially useful, not only to remedy patient flow issues, but also to prevent them occurring in the first instance. This means that reactivation campaigns should be undertaken routinely. I suggest a monthly reactivation program. In that way you keep on top of your database and prevent the deterioration of your most important asset.

There are other specific times when reactivation campaigns are useful. For instance, when a practice is sold, a lot of the value is in the database. For the purchasing dentist, it is important to achieve the best possible return on their investment and one of the ways of doing this is to ensure that there are as many active patients as possible.

I have recently purchased an established practice in Canberra. It is a well-established practice with pretty good patient flow. However, like the practice I referred to earlier, the recall system had not been properly set up and we have over 1000 patients on the database who are not on the recall system. Some of them have not been seen in over five years. Literally, as I type this manuscript, I have my staff reactivating as many patients as possible from that list.

Other than generally trying to increase patient flow (and maintain good business practices), reactivation campaigns are also useful when a practice is trying to establish a hygiene department or when completing a purge of old patient charts.

The main thing with a reactivation campaign is to reactivate as early as possible. The longer a person has been away from the practice, the weaker the relationship between the practice and your patient, and the harder it is to re-activate them.

How to Conduct a Successful Reactivation Campaign

There are several steps to conducting a reactivation campaign. The first step is to get an accurate list of the patients requiring reactivation. As I mentioned earlier, reports for patients with overdue recalls and outstanding treatment can be printed from your practice management software.

The list is then sorted and segmented based on the recency of their interaction with the practice. We look to reactivate those patients who have most recently interacted with the practice first because we know they'll be easier to reactivate than patients who have been "missing in action" for longer periods. By starting here we achieve maximum return for effort as well as ensuring that more recent inactive patients don't become long-term inactive patients.

In our practice, we prepare a letter for each patient and post it via traditional mail. We use a mailing house to send this letter. This letter will vary from one practice to another but in our case, we simply apologised for the fact we had not been in touch more regularly and outlined our philosophy of care before inviting them to return to the practice for their next appointment. We also indicated that we would contact them by telephone in the following week to discuss the situation.

The letter is then followed up with a phone call to the patient within one week of the letter being sent. The timing of this phone call is critical. The call needs to occur while the letter is still fresh in the mind of the patient and emphasise that we do what we say we'll do in the letter.

The phone call has several components to it. These are:

1. The dentist and I have been reviewing your file.

2. Last time you were in, Dr Green diagnosed a ... The aim is to focus only on incomplete treatment here and build a sense of importance for that treatment to be completed.

3. The dentist was concerned and asked me to give you a call to schedule an appointment.

4. Offer an appointment time using a series of alternative choices.

5. Book the appointment and gain a commitment.

6. An example of such a conversation might be:

Receptionist: "Hello Mrs Smith, this is Mary from Dr Green's surgery. How are you today?"

Mrs Smith: Well thank you."

Receptionist: "Dr Green and I were reviewing your file yesterday. We noted that although the root canal on the lower right molar has been completed, the tooth has not yet been crowned as had been planned. Although the root canal treatment may have alleviated the pain and infection, the tooth is heavily filled and prone to breaking. If the tooth does break it could result in the loss of that tooth. Dr Green was concerned so he asked me to give you a call to schedule a short follow up appointment to check on the tooth."

Mrs Smith: "Well the tooth is quite comfortable but that should be OK."

Receptionist: "Mrs Smith, are there any days that work better for you?"

Mrs Smith: "I prefer a Monday or a Tuesday because I have commitments on the other days of the week."

Receptionist: "And do you prefer morning or afternoon appointments?"

Mrs Smith: "Morning"

Receptionist: "OK, I have Monday at 10am or Tuesday at 11am. Which of those suits you best?"

Mrs Smith: "Monday at 10am"

Receptionist: "OK, I have you scheduled to see Dr Green at 10am on Monday the 3rd of March. So we'll see you then? " (Asked with a smile and a light tone. This is designed to achieve an appointment commitment from the patient.)

Mrs Smith: "Yes, I'll be there. It's in my diary."

Receptionist: "That's great Mrs Smith. I'll let Dr Green know to expect you on Monday 3rd March at 10am."

Mrs Smith: "I'll see you then. Bye for now"

Receptionist: "Bye Mrs Smith"

As with all marketing initiatives, the key is to track progress. We keep a spreadsheet that details when the letter was sent, when calls were made, any emails sent as well as the response from the patient with any of these interactions.

We have found in our own practice that the reactivation success rate is currently 21%. This might not seem high but it means that we now have over two hundred patients booked in for appointments that were previously lost to us. Of course, reactivation rates will be higher the earlier you reactivate and also on the quality of the relationship you had with the patient before they became inactive.

Word of Mouth Marketing

Wouldn't it be nice to have a constant stream of great new patients who already trust you and who come to your practice ready to accept treatment? The most common problem I am asked to solve is that of patient flow. The good news is that with effective word-of-mouth marketing, you can experience both of these things. Word-of-mouth marketing is inexpensive – virtually free.

In any business, the best new customer is one who has been referred by a happy, existing customer. I am amazed that so many practice owners get so caught up in the hype of the latest marketing tactic that they forget that their best source of new patients is right under their noses. What's needed is a way to mobilise this latent sales force.

Dentists will generally accept a referral and be grateful for it, however, that's where it seems to end. Most don't have a structured system for encouraging existing patients to refer others. This is absolutely crazy and is costing literally tens of thousands, if not hundreds of thousands of dollars in lost production.

Word-of-mouth marketing can grow a practice exponentially in a very short period of time. Not only does it grow your practice, it also improves the quality of your patient base. Let's think about that for a moment.

Wouldn't it be terrific if you could clone your best patients? The old saying that, *"birds of a feather flock together"*, is pretty true in my experience.

Let's assume you have a patient database of two thousand patients. Of those patients, let's say 50% are the sort of patients you enjoy treating. That means that there are one thousand patients in your practice who have family and friends you'd more than likely enjoy treating as well.

Now let's consider your sphere of influence. How many people do you know well enough to say "hello" to and have a conversation with? Ten? Twenty? Thirty? One hundred?

In his book, *The Tipping Point* [19.] Malcolm Gladwell examined the process of creating a social epidemic. He conducted one particular experiment where he selected random names out of the New York telephone directory and asked subjects how many people they knew with the names from the random list. Different cohorts had different results but on average, they knew about forty people each. These results were based on an incomplete list of names from the New York phone book.

For the sake of our argument, let's assume that the thousand patients we mentioned earlier, each have the potential to refer forty high quality, new patients to your practice. Even if you halved the sphere of influence, the numbers are impressive, but not only that, each of these new patients has their own sphere of influence, which will generate even more referrals.

Start by setting a referral ratio goal for your practice. The referral ratio is the number of new patients generated through word-of-mouth marketing, divided by the number of existing patients. For example, if I had one hundred patients in my practice, and I generated twenty referrals, my referral ratio would be 20%.

You can then break down the annual goal into smaller monthly and weekly goals. It is imperative that you know your numbers, be accountable and be consistent.

Given the competition dentists are facing and will continue to face, it is imperative that practices have a low-cost way of generating high quality, new patients. Practices that do this will drastically outperform those that don't. It is as simple as that.

ESAR: The 4-Step Method to Generating Referrals

I use a four-step process for generating word-of-mouth referrals. This process provides a framework from which practices can generate high quality, qualified, new patients at will. It is represented by the acronym ESAR, which stands for: Earning the referral, Setting expectations, Asking for the referral and Rewarding the referral. This system was created by modifying and adding to Dan Kennedy's three-step EAR system[20].

Earn the Referral by Delivering Wow Customer Service

Satisfied customers are a dime a dozen. Being satisfied essentially means that the customer got what they paid for and the transaction occurred without anything to report. The simple truth is that a satisfied customer doesn't refer plentifully.

If the ultimate aim is to create a constant stream of high quality referrals, then you need to surprise and delight patients to the extent that they have a story to go away and tell their families and friends. The experience needs to be a "Wow! How did you do that?" kind of experience. Wowing your patients is the basis of both patient retention, as well as generating word-of-mouth referrals.

I have covered the concept of giving patients a great experience in detail in Chapter 5. However, it is worth repeating that because patients can't really judge our technical abilities, they form an opinion as to how "good" we are based on proxies that they can observe, such as how well they felt cared for, the way they interact with staff, the cleanliness of the practice and so on. Therefore, we need to "Wow" patients in ways that matter to them.

The opinion a patient forms about our abilities may or may not be correct. However, the patient's perception is their reality and determines whether or not they will refer family and friends. With this in mind, it is important that nothing is left to chance. A "Wow" patient experience does not happen by accident. It is choreographed from start to finish.

I suggest you look at every interaction the patient has with your practice and look at ways to connect with and surprise and delight your patient at each of those touch-points. Make sure you complete the action steps in Chapter 5 if you have not already done so.

Set Expectations

Many years ago when I was a dentist in the Navy, I spent quite a bit of time at sea. It really was a lot of fun as a young dentist. We worked hard and played harder. When the sea state was rough the ship would roll around and it was impossible to do any dentistry safely. During those times I'd go and hang out with the ship's company and see how the rest of the ship operated – learning how everyone had a role in keeping the ship operational.

It was a great eye-opener and I met a lot of characters. On one ship I had the role of being a "Divisional Officer" for a group of sailors which basically meant I was responsible for the welfare of these men. One day, a Leading Seaman came to see me about going on a training course to further his skills. When we looked at the courses available, there were several that were suitable. One of the available courses was also a pre-requisite for promotion to the next rank, Petty Officer. I suggested he enrol in that course as it met his training needs and he could also use it to ready himself for promotion.

I was surprised when he indicated that he didn't really want to be promoted and was happy to stay a Leading Seaman. In my naivety I tried to explain the benefits of promotion to him – an opportunity to lead others, more responsibility and so on. It turns out that the Leading Seaman didn't want to lead other people and was happy with the level of responsibility he had.

What I realised during that exchange, is that some people like to lead and others like to be led. One is not necessarily better than the other. However, up until then (the ripe old age of twenty-five), I had assumed that because I wanted to be a leader, so too did everyone else.

My boss at sea was the Executive Officer (XO) who is the second in charge of the ship. Although I didn't spend a lot of time in his company, he helped me distil another lesson from the discussion with the Leading Seaman. When I recounted the conversation, he didn't seem surprised by what had transpired. He then asked me if I wanted to be promoted and take on more responsibility. When I indicated I did, he simply said my role was to lead those looking for leadership in whatever environment I found myself in.

These lessons have stayed with me over the years. When I left the Navy and entered practice, I realised that patients like to be led too.

If our ultimate aim is to create a patient-driven sales force, then it makes sense to lead our patients through that process.

When I left the Navy to enter private practice I must admit that I felt uncertain of myself. After having lived and worked in such a regimented environment, I found the lack of rules a little hard to adjust to.

Patients seemed to like me (as much as I could tell) but I was not getting busier and had holes in my appointment book. As the months went by, I felt demoralised and even wondered about returning to the security of the Navy.

My first boss out of the Navy had a very successful practice and was always busy with patients. Her patients loved her and would always refer their family and friends to her. I decided that I would eavesdrop on what she said to patients to see if some of her "magic" could rub off on me.

As I listened from the room next door, I couldn't believe what I heard. As she was talking to a new patient, she said something that reminded me of the lesson I'd learned from the Leading Seaman years earlier and taught me, simultaneously, a new lesson as well.

"Mr Smith, welcome to our practice. We're really pleased to see you here." The conversation went on and then she said something that struck me. *"As your friend Susie would have mentioned, we are a referral-based practice. Our philosophy is to provide comprehensive treatment that lasts and lasts.*

So that we can continue to provide the level of service that our patients have come to expect from us, we need a constant source of new patients. Can I ask for your help? At the end of the appointment, I'm going to ask how you found today's appointment. I'm then going to ask that if you enjoyed your experience with us, you refer your family and friends to see us. Is that OK with you?"

What my boss had done was illustrate two very important lessons to me. Firstly, she had asked for help and secondly, she had set the expectation of referring family and friends to the practice. Those two lessons, combined with the lesson from the Navy, formed the basis of setting the scene to generate word-of-mouth referrals.

What do I mean by that? Over the years I discovered that I could expect more from patients than I thought possible. I also learned that if they like you, they're very willing to help you. The key message is that they need to know that you actually want help and then how to go about providing it.

It took me a while to refine this system of setting the scene. I knew what I had wanted to achieve, but just couldn't figure out a neat way of doing it. There was a lot of trial and error – more error than trial, to be frank.

One day I was listening to an audio programme by another marketer, Jay Abraham, who was talking about the use of a customer charter as a marketing tool. He described how it outlined the rights and obligations of the customer and the business and that it could be used to set the tone for the way they would interact. The seed of an idea was planted, however, it was not until I went to the bank to open a new account, that I received a document outlining the covenant between the bank and the customer, that the idea was really cemented.

I took the idea of creating a Customer Charter and made my own. It outlined what I felt was a fair deal for both the practice and the patient; explaining the rights and obligations of both parties. One of the obligations of the patient was that if they enjoyed their experience at the practice (and only if), I needed them to refer at least one patient of equal quality as themselves to the practice. Like my boss before me, I explained that our philosophy was to provide comprehensive, definitive treatment, and that as such, we needed a constant supply of new patients in order to remain viable and continue to provide the level of care our patients came to expect from us.

The Patient Covenant, as I like to call it, explains what we think represents a fair deal and sets expectations at the outset.

I must admit that I thought my plan was a bit audacious and could potentially offend some patients. What I found, however, was that the opposite was true. Not only did patients not take offence, they actually embraced the idea. Some even asked if they could refer more than one .

I send out this Patient Covenant in my New Patient Pack, along with the usual welcome letter, privacy policy and so on.*

Asking

There are countless theories and literally hundreds of books on how to go about asking for the referral. I like to keep things pretty simple when I ask for one. However, there are a few guidelines that will increase the success of your referral process.

Like most dentists, I was originally averse to the idea of actually asking a patient to send their family and friends. But I realised that if I didn't ask, it wouldn't happen. So I steeled myself and just asked.

My first attempts were horrible. I felt awkward, I stumbled over my words and I beat around the bush, trying to ask in a subtle, obtuse way. Needless to say, I wasn't too successful. What I did have in my favour, however, was a stubborn nature and I vowed to persevere.

According to some psychologists and trainers, it can take up to ninety times of practise before a new task is effectively learned and ingrained. What I found to be of great help was to role-play the process in staff meetings or with a couple of close friends. By doing so, I did as many of the ninety repetitions in a "safe" environment before being let loose on the patients. In this way, I was able to be more confident when asking patients to refer their families and friends.

I also realised that there are better times to ask for a referral than others. I realised that patients were most impressed with our service when they experienced it for the first handful of times. The patients were in a state of "Wow" and remarking on the fact that our practice was like no other they had experienced.

---

* While I was having my epiphany, I was unaware that this concept had already been pioneered in dentistry by Paddi Lund who built an exclusive, referral-only practice in Brisbane, Australia. While the concept of a patient covenant may not be new, it is massively effective.

As I mentioned in Chapter 5, one of my favourite coffee shops in Brisbane is a place called "Espresso Republic." Not only is the coffee great, but the crew there remember my name and my coffee order. When I first went there, I was really impressed with the coffee and level of service and I couldn't stop raving about the place. When I went back a little later, I was still impressed but not as 'Wowed' because I had come to expect that level of service. It is the same with all service industries. So it follows that while the patient is at their happiest with us is the moment that we ask for the referral.

My view is to be pretty up front when asking for the referral. I typically say some thing like *"Mrs Smith, as you know, our practice has been built mainly through word-of-mouth recommendations and we don't like to take just any new patient. We enjoy looking after you and if you have any family or friends that you feel would like to come along, we'd be happy to look after them on your behalf."*

I have chosen the words in that phrase carefully. Not only are we asking for the referral but we are building an element of exclusivity onto the referral by indicating we don't take any old Joe off the street. We're looking to attract more of our ideal type of patients – those who believe what we believe.

Tools for Asking for Referrals

Some people like to use a variety of tools to ask for referrals. They might use a "care to share" card, which is essentially an invitation your patient can give to family or friends. Others like to use "Viva" cards (see viva-concepts. com), which are similar to "care to share" cards, but have an in-built tracking system to ensure each new patient is attributed to a particular referrer. In that way, you can determine who your best referrers are.

"Care to share" cards and "Viva" cards are often used in conjunction with an offer, although they don't necessarily have to be used in that way.

Personally, I don't attach an offer or inducement with my referral requests because I am looking to build exclusivity, and the inclusion of a financial incentive is counter to how I want to position my practice. However, you will need to determine what works best in your market and make your decision accordingly. If you do offer an incentive to visit your practice, you should be well-acquainted with the value of each new patient in dollar terms to ensure that the cost of acquisition does not exceed the value of the patient.

Reward

A short story: I am a neat freak. I live in a family that is not as concerned with tidiness as I am. My eldest daughter is particularly messy. When I have asked her to clean up, my requests tend to fall on deaf ears. In the past, I'd get so frustrated with the mess, I'd clean it up myself. Half-an-hour later, it would be messy again. I needed a new approach. We set up a "star chart" where she would get a star each day her room was tidy. When fourteen stars were accumulated, she received some pocket money that she could spend on whatever she liked. After just a week of this, I didn't have to remind her to clean up her room any more.

For anyone with children, you will know that behaviour that is rewarded is repeated: the same holds true for patients who refer their family and friends to the practice.

Recognising the referral is critical. In essence that patient has given you a gift and it is common courtesy to acknowledge the gift and say "thank-you."

Again, there are many different schools of thought about how to recognise and thank patients for referring friends and family. I feel that the nature of the recognition ought to be consistent with how the referral was asked for in the first place.

For instance, if your patient has referred their friends to you as an act of faith and genuinely wanting to help your practice or their friend, a discount coupon can cheapen the whole transaction. In some instances, it may even offend the referrer. In these instances, a hand-written note of appreciation goes a long way.

However, if you have asked for the referral by giving a "care-to-share" card with an offer attached, then a physical gift or "dental dollars" might be more appropriate. If you do give a gift, then ensure the gift is commensurate with the nature of the referral. So the lesson when deciding whether or not to give gifts, comes down to knowing your market, as well as being congruent with how the referral was asked for in the first place.

A Note to Specialists

Building a Tribe for dental specialists is a little more complex than for a general practitioner. When I speak to specialists, I find that most of them accept patients with or without a referral from another practitioner.

While the principles I have described in this chapter have been written from the perspective of serving patients as the customer, they apply to any customer – patients or referring practitioners.

As you go through the Action Steps, you will need to complete the tasks from each perspective. When it comes to your referral base you will need to determine which practitioners have stopped referring. What protocol will you develop to re-activate them? How can you implement the ESAR protocol to increase patient flow as a result of increased referrals from patients and referring practitioners?

Building a robust referral network is an integral part of the overall marketing plan for a specialist practice. There are many specific marketing measures beyond the scope of this book, that are at the disposal of specialists. If you'd like more information, please email me at **hello@drjessegreen.com**

Action Steps

1. Check your practice management system so that the recall fields are correctly set for each and every patient. This prevents patient loss by mismanaging the database. It's important to know your software!

2. Print a list of current patients who have been sent recalls but who have not made an appointment then follow them up with a phone call. If they're busy, schedule an agreed time to call back. Again, script the call and brainstorm any objections that may need to be overcome.

3. Print, sort and segment a list of inactive patients and create a multi-step reactivation protocol (e.g. initial letter, follow up phone call and email).

4. Implement a Reactivation Campaign starting with those patients who have been in for an appointment most recently.

5. Draft each step of the ESAR protocol and implement it.

Remember, it can take up to ninety times for a new skill to be integrated. Once scripted, rehearse conversations in a safe environment by role-playing with staff during your weekly team meeting.

Download the Workbook

Remember to download the companion workbook to access checklists, cheat sheets and other resources. It is available at:
www.drjessegreen.com/retention/workbook

9

THE POWER OF AN ELITE TEAM

A team isn't a bunch of kids out to win. A team is something you belong to, something you feel, something you have to earn.

—

Gordon Bombay
The Mighty Ducks, 1992

THE POWER OF
AN ELITE TEAM

At first glance, the discussion of the power of an elite team might seem out of place in a book about patient retention. However, running a successful enterprise is a team sport and the success of the business is directly proportional to the performance of the team.

The simple truth is that it is impossible to do it all yourself. It is a folly to try. Staff free you up to do what you do best – whether it be clinical dentistry as the practitioner within the business or as the entrepreneur working on the business rather than in it.

There are many benefits to having a team that performs at the highest level. Usually, most attention is drawn to the leverage it affords and improvements in productivity and morale. While these are critical, little, if any, discussion is given to the essential role staff play in customer retention.

Having staff, or team members who perform at a high level, is essential to the running of a dental practice. This chapter focuses on the role of staff in patient retention as well how to attract and retain elite team members.

Retain Staff, Retain Patients

When I first began in practice I had quite a few issues with staff turnover. I had taken over the day-to-day running of the practice from my wife and the team that she had assembled really loved and respected her.

I have a different personality and style from my wife, and I found that after a short period, the staff were openly rebelling, being discourteous and disrespectful. It wasn't all their fault though. I was learning the ropes and making mistakes as I went.

At one point, it seemed that there was a revolving door as staff came and went with alarming regularity. I had one cheeky friend who used to telephone me weekly to see who'd resigned that week. The challenge was brought acutely into focus when patients noticed that they had a new dental assistant each visit and commented that I must have been hard to work with. A few patients even left the practice.

At that time my focus was primarily on the patients, trying to give them the best experience possible. But I was operating like a one-man band, trying to be all things to all people. I was constantly reacting rather than responding. I was exhausted.

It gradually dawned on me that if I could find a way to attract high-quality staff and retain them, not only would I achieve boosts in productivity, improved clinical outcomes and improved personal and professional satisfaction, I would also retain my patient base.

Over time, I learned that rather than dedicating all of my attention to patients, I was better advised to focus more on my staff and empower them to focus on the patients. I decided to treat my staff as my internal customer and worked hard at nurturing my relationship with them.

The business model shifted from my trying to do everything, to focussing on supporting the team. We began to view our patients as customers rather than patients. We felt that we do things *for* customers but do things *to* patients. This simple change in terminology meant we really positioned ourselves as a service business. The team supported the customer, the customer supported the business and the business supported me.

By making my staff my internal customers, not only did we retain staff, we retained patients. What's more, team morale skyrocketed, productivity and profitability increased and in the process, I was freed from feeling the need to do it all myself.

Patient Relationships With Staff

Some time ago I was a consultant to a law firm on the topic of marketing and it became apparent that they had a particularly profitable account with a nearby local council. What became apparent on further investigation was that this multi-million dollar relationship hinged on the personal relationship between one of the partners of the law firm and a key person within the council. If the person within the council moved for any reason, then the business relationship between the firm and the council would be in jeopardy.

The strategy we recommended for the law firm was to have more of their people get to know more people within the council. Specifically, however, we looked to build multiple relationships at every level within the council structure with multiple people within the law firm, so that in the event that a key person from either the firm or the council moved on, the business relationship would remain intact.

The same principle applies to a dental practice. Having more than one relationship between the practice and the patient ensures more deposits are made into the "emotional bank account" of the patient, so that if something does go awry, the account balance can cope and the relationship endures.

It might be a knock to one's ego to find that there are some patients who visit certain dental practices not necessarily because of the relationship they have with the dentists, but rather, as a result of the relationship they have with the staff. While it is true that all staff can develop relationships with patients, it is especially true for the staff who have the most interaction with the patients in the absence of the dentist, namely the dental hygienist (or therapist) and the reception staff. It is absolutely true that dental assistants can also develop these relationships but in my experience, they tend to need to be cultivated more deliberately by the assistant, actively engaging the patient or by redefining their role to that of a "care nurse" or "patient co-ordinator" who ushers the patient through every aspect of the appointment.

I was recently talking to a friend of mine, Sacha, and we were discussing the relationship he has with his dentist. I was very interested to note that he visits the dental practice because of the relationship he has with the dental hygienist. It turns out that Sacha is ambivalent about the dentist but really enjoys the level of care he receives from the hygienist. I don't know the dentist, but if he is sensible he should be delighted with this outcome and should be actively trying to retain his hygienist. Clearly his hygienist has an ability to develop happy patient relationships independently of him and the hygienist is now an additional "rainmaker" for the business.

As it stands though, the relationship between Sacha and the hygienist represents a single point of failure. Should the hygienist leave, it is conceivable that Sacha will too. Clearly, the dentist should also be trying to develop his own relationship with Sacha to cement his loyalty to the practice.

From a retention perspective, practices are well served if multiple team members develop relationships with as many members of a family as possible – more of our people relating to more of your people – just like the law firm I mentioned earlier.

By encouraging staff to develop their own relationships with patients, an environment is created where the relationship between the practice and patient becomes more intertwined, meaning patients are far more likely to stay at the practice.

Attributes of an Elite Team

It may be a sporting cliché, but there is some truth to the notion that a champion team will outperform a team of champions every day. The strength of a team is derived from, and is greater than, the sum of its parts (the individual members of the team). The same holds true for business.

When we look to recruit for our business, there are many skills and attributes we're looking for in the applicants. As I'll discuss shortly, in my practice we use a profiling system to uncover the key strengths of an applicant to ensure their strengths match those required for the position. In essence, we ensure the applicant is in a role that plays to their natural strengths and talents.

There are four personal qualities I look for, no matter what role an applicant is applying for.

1. Culture Fit

I wrote in Chapter 3 that inspiring leaders and companies start with "why". They have a clear vision of the experience they want to create for their patient. A good vision statement is bold, empowering and inspiring. The vision is typically supported by a series of values or beliefs that reflect the ethos of the company.

In his book, The Apple Experience, Carmine Gallo tells us that when applicants apply for a retail job at Apple, they're applying to be part of something larger than just the job.[21] From Apple's perspective, they need to be sure that the potential employee is a culture fit. The whole recruiting process is designed to uncover the core values and beliefs of the applicant to ensure that an appropriate person is hired.

The values, beliefs and vision of the staff who do eventually get to work at Apple are aligned with those of the company. They love their work environment and feel that they are part of something exciting.

A clear vision is very alluring. It is not just Apple employees who want to feel they're part of something bigger. Nearly everyone wants to feel that they are making a difference and contributing to a higher purpose.

The same holds true for all businesses, including dental practices. Imagine how your practice would look and feel if you have a team of A-Grade players who were committed to the vision of the practice? How much would your patients love coming to see you? How much would you love going to work every day? I can guarantee that you and your team will perform to a level that you would rarely, if ever, have experienced before.

2. Courtesy

When I was a young boy growing up, my father would always say, "Manners maketh the man, Jesse". He believed society to be the richer when everyone treated each other with courtesy and respect. It's funny how we turn into our parents sometimes, and now that I'm a parent, I try hard to instil those values into my own children.

But what does this have to with dentistry? Everything. We spend our day interacting with people from start to finish and for me, this is one of the parts of dentistry I enjoy the most: pleasant social interactions make me feel happy and connected to my patients.

In our fast-paced digital world, where even abbreviations get abbreviated, it seems simple courtesies are dispensed with for the sake of rapid communication. It's ironic that we expect our children to be polite and have good manners and yet we fire off a one line email devoid of a salutation without giving it a second thought.

While I might sound like I'm on a one-man crusade, it is my belief that when we are polite and courteous to those with whom we interact, the exchange is more pleasant and we feel happier too.

I have said that while we view our team as family, we also like to view our patients as very dear friends. That's why we have a few house rules when it comes to manners. We believe that in all of our interactions, we should use "please" and "thank-you", and remembering that addressing people by name is one of the most basic courtesies we can observe. Call me old-fashioned, but I still use an honorific when I meet people for the first time – especially elderly patients. I continue to use it until they tell me not to. We tell the truth, and if a mistake is made we own up to it, apologise and make amends. If we are busy with one patient and another arrives, we acknowledge the second patient and let them know we'll attend to them as soon as we can. Are we perfect all the time? Of course not, but by having these rules, we at least know what we're aiming for.

It's not rocket science but these simple courtesies improve our interactions and make us all feel happier. There is no subtext or ulterior marketing motive, it is just a case of human beings trying to treat others as we'd like to be treated ourselves.

3. Telling the Truth and Doing the Right Thing

When I was ten years old my family moved to Papua New Guinea and after a year of schooling in Port Moresby, I returned to Brisbane to attend boarding school. My House Master was a man called Mick Roche-Kelly. Mick had spent time in the Merchant Navy and was a wise and kindly older man.

Mr. Roche-Kelly and his family lived in a flat under our dormitory. The noise must have been like living under a bowling alley! One night, some of us were jumping on and off beds and playing rugby in the middle of the dorm and we were making a terrible din. An angry voice was heard over the ruckus and we knew that in a moment or two he'd be up the stairs. Mick burst in as we tried to scuttle away quickly – we'd been caught.

We all had to stand in a line and the offenders were asked to step forward. Needless to say, those of us involved felt a sense of trepidation as we stepped forward. Those who did were punished by being sent to bed without supper. There were a few who did not confess, however, and got off scot free – for a while. I never did find out how he knew, but Mr. Roche-Kelly made sure that those boys received a more stern punishment than the rest of us, because they'd lied.

The following day, we were all sat down and had a chat about honesty and integrity – the importance of telling the truth when it isn't convenient – in essence, doing the right thing.

The same holds true in our practices. There will be times when it is tempting to tell a small lie or to do something just a teeny bit dishonest in order to get something done or to alleviate an uncomfortable situation. One of our "house rules" is that we tell the truth, no matter how uncomfortable it may be, and we face the consequences and make amends, if that is what is required.

We had a situation where a patient had rung for an appointment. As the call came in there were other things happening at the reception desk and in the confusion the appointment was not entered in the appointment book. When the patient arrived for her appointment, we simply did not have a vacancy that we could offer her.

In truth, we had had some issues with our server and we could have easily blamed the error on that rather than "fessing up" about our mistake. In the end, and to her eternal credit, the receptionist owned up and admitted the error. While the patient wasn't super happy that she had been inconvenienced, she appreciated the honesty and took the view that "we all make mistakes". The patient stayed for a cup of tea and in the end she and the receptionist were having a good chat. The fact that the problem was resolved so well was simply due to not trying to hide the mistake, or blaming anyone else – the mistake was admitted and rectified.

In a small way, that episode has turned into a positive because the cup of tea and chat she had with the patient helped create a relationship and that patient keeps on coming to the practice.

4. Communication

Relating to and connecting with others is at the heart of all we do in our practice – and indeed in life. The ability to communicate effectively with others is essential to foster moments of connection. There is a saying that we *"have two ears and one mouth – use them in that proportion."* I have found that the best communicators are also the best listeners.

Listening, to me, is different from hearing. Listening is about truly being present and picking up on the non-verbal communication as much as what is said.

By actively listening to patients we get to understand what is most important to them. Knowing what the patient really wants (or does not want) is the critical first step to developing a relationship with them and then serving them better.

Hiring Process

As we have become better at making our staff our internal customer, we have also worked hard to attract high quality people to our team. In the early years, our recruitment was hit-and-miss and poor recruitment contributed to our staff turnover. I soon realised I needed a more predictable way of recruiting high calibre staff.

To assist in that process, I developed a checklist for recruiting staff which has been refined over the years. It has ten points that outlines the process that I follow when recruiting staff.

As I mentioned earlier, my aim is to have staff in a position that plays to their natural strengths and talents. In the past, I found that I had recruited people I thought would be perfect for a role, only to find out they were not. On some occasions, I found that applicants were even able to modify their behaviour for a period of time, but whether they modified it deliberately, to get the job, I'm not sure. However, the result was that when their behaviour returned to its normal state (which it always does because behaviour is driven by our psychology), I found I had a staff member who was not ideal for the role.

Because human behaviour is largely driven by our subconscious, I was looking for a way to examine the individual strengths of a candidate, at a psychological level. Some time ago, I came across the concept of psychological profiling as a means of vetting applicants. We now compare the profile of the applicant against the profile of known high-performers in similar roles, and have found that we had a greater success recruiting staff who were primarily suited to a particular role. Since then, profiling applicants has become an integral part of my recruiting process.

Training and Induction

Zappos.com is the world's largest online retailer of shoes with an annual turnover in excess of $1 billion. It is renowned for being a purpose-driven company – to deliver happiness through outstanding customer service.

According to Zappos CEO, Tony Hseih, a large measure of their success comes from the fact that their purpose, or their "why", is underpinned by a set of core values and a culture that informs everything they do, so in order to understand why values and culture are so fundamental to Zappos's success, it is worth understanding a little of Tony Hseih's history.

Hseih is no stranger to success. After graduating from Harvard in 1995, he co-founded a company called Link Exchange in 1996. Over the following three years, it grew rapidly, culminating in its sale to Microsoft for a reported $265 million.

In his book, Delivering Happiness,[8] Hseih makes the point that Link Exchange grew so rapidly that they lost control of their culture. At the peak of their growth, their need to fill roles was so great that their recruitment was frenetic and haphazard. Not surprisingly, their haphazard recruiting led to poor recruiting decisions.

Because Link Exchange had not set out to create a culture with specific intent nor to protect it, the culture that did exist deteriorated to the point that Hseih no longer enjoyed going to work. Ultimately, his unhappiness was so great that he decided to prematurely leave the company following its sale to Microsoft. Even though he incurred a huge financial penalty, Hseih knew that he could not stay.

When he joined Zappos, Hseih was determined not to make the same mistakes. He realised that as the company grew, it was vital that it stayed true to its values and culture. As such, Zappos has developed both recruiting and training processes that place values and culture at the front and centre of the company. It has been this obsession with culture and values that has been largely responsible for the growth of Zappos into a billion dollar enterprise.

Implementation

I have already spoken of the need to recruit employees whose values align with those of the practice and who are also a great culture fit. The recruitment process should be designed in such a manner as to test these values to ensure that they are aligned with the values and vision of the practice.

Similarly, the induction process is designed to reinforce those values. At Zappos, no matter what position or department you are recruited to, all employees undergo an induction process. Zappos is so serious about maintaining its culture that it recognises that from time-to-time, a mis-hire can occur. Recognising this, during the induction process, they offer the employees $1000 to leave (on top of the salary they would normally receive). With such a large and unique company and culture, it is inevitable that some people will slip through the recruiting net and Zappos does need a way to maintain the integrity of its culture within its company.

When I speak to a lot of dentists, they feel that they're too busy to implement such a system and it's a bit over the top. While I understand that the day-to-day rigours of running a dental practice (I run one too!), most of the dentists who are "too busy" to implement this are the same ones who whinge about their staff.

An induction or training process need not be a four-week course as it is at Zappos, but at the very least the practice needs to have a structured training pipeline that includes both technical training and elements that include the vision for the practice. In our practice, we have developed a training chart that categorises individual tasks into key areas such as values, clinical systems, administrative systems, customer service and so on. Over a twelve-week period, we systematically induct the staff member into each of our processes and where necessary, provide the appropriate training.

A large part of our induction and processes focus on how we operate our practice. We focus on being "on purpose" rather than simply being "on task", because how the task is completed will greatly influence the outcome of the activity.

Without taking a systemised approach, there is little hope of the team performing to its full capacity or the practice fulfilling its potential.

Performance Management

Author, Jim Collins, says *"the enemy of great is good."*[22] As the team matures, the biggest risk is complacency. It is critical for all businesses to constantly innovate and improve because if you're not improving, you're stagnating.

A key area that drives our continual improvement programme is timely and accurate reporting. We regularly review the performance of the business in general and the staff in particular.

Treating staff as our internal customer does not mean we should be accepting of anything less than their best. All people slip up, make mistakes and can lose focus. That is to be human. What's important, however, is that as a team we regularly refocus our efforts and constantly improve.

I prefer not to use performance reviews as a stick but rather, as a carrot. I want to find out how we can help staff grow and reach their potential and what resources are required to bring this improvement to fruition. Performance reviews are closely related to the staff members' job descriptions. The outcomes are mutually agreed upon and we reconvene regularly to check progress.

Broadly, I focus on five key areas:

1. What do you think you're doing well?

2. What areas need improvement?

3. What resources are needed for improvement and can the practice provide these?

4. How do we measure success?

5. What outcomes are agreed upon?

I ask the staff-member to ponder these questions prior to our meeting and I do too. Typically, staff are aware of how they're performing and usually their responses to the questions above are very similar to mine.

In the event a staff member is not performing well, we have that discussion early and try to uncover what lies behind the slip in performance. From there, we can develop a plan to help that staff member at least regain but preferably improve upon their previous level of performance.

During these changing times, a commitment to continual improvement is essential in the quest to build a successful practice and managing the performance of staff is fundamental to that process.

Action Steps

1. Download the companion workbook from www.drjessegreen.com/retention/workbook and take note of the recruitment checklist.

2. Develop a training and induction protocol for each position within the practice. (If you don't have position descriptions and an organisational chart, you will need to complete these first.)

3. Develop and implement a protocol for managing performance with a view to getting the best from staff, and creating an environment of continuous improvement.

Download the Workbook

Remember to download the companion workbook to access checklists, cheat sheets and other resources. It is available at:
www.drjessegreen.com/retention/workbook

10

BRINGING IT ALL TOGETHER

Sow a thought and you reap an action; sow an act and you reap a habit; sow a habit and you reap a character; sow a character and you reap a destiny.

—

Ralph Waldo Emerson

BRINGING
IT ALL TOGETHER

Retaining patients is one of the fundamental activities of a successful practice. In the previous chapters, I have built a case for the importance of patient retention through loyalty. You now have a blueprint to protect and grow your most important business asset in any economy. However, there is still a piece of the puzzle missing and that piece is implementation.

By the end of this chapter, you will have the necessary tools to implement the information you have already received. The power of information is not so much in its knowledge but in its application. It is the application of knowledge that really separates the successful practices from the rest.

The material in this chapter will help you crystallise what it is you really want to accomplish and sets you on a path to achieve success according to your definition.

Setting Goals

Why do some people achieve so much while others meander through life achieving very little? The answer lies in the power of setting a goal. In his book, *What they don't teach you at Harvard Business School,* author, Mark McCormack, discusses a study where MBA students were asked, "Have you set clear, written goals for your future and made plans to accomplish them?" Three percent (3%) of the students had written goals, thirteen percent (13%) had goals that had not been written down while eighty-four percent (84%) had not set any goal at all.

McCormack reports that ten years after graduation these students, now in the workforce, were re-surveyed and the results were illuminating. The thirteen percent (13%) who had goals earned twice as much as those who did not set goals at all. However, the three percent who had written goals earned ten times as much as the remaining ninety-seven percent (97%) combined.[23]

Goal-setting is recognised as a common trait of successful people the world over, regardless of their endeavour. In fact, it would be difficult to point to a person who has achieved notable success without first having set the goal to do so.

That's because a goal defines what success means for a given individual. Arnold Schwarzenegger, Steve Jobs, Richard Branson, Oprah Winfrey, Madonna and Jim Carrey have all, at various times in their careers, advocated the use of goals as a method of achieving what they want from life.

What is it that makes setting goals so powerful? Setting goals stimulates the reticular activation system (RAS) within the human brain. The RAS acts as a filter, bringing relevant information into mental focus and moving information not relevant to the pursuit of the goal out of focus. The RAS narrows your attention allowing you to focus on what really matters.

So how do we set goals in a way that maximises the chance of attaining them? Below are seven steps to effective goal achievement:

1. Set specific goals. Have absolute clarity about what you want to achieve. Define the goal precisely using metrics. Rather than setting the goal to "lose weight" you might set the goal to be 81kg with 15 per cent body fat.

2. Understand the motivation behind the goal. The motivation must be strong enough to keep you committed when times get tough. Set goals you really care about.

3. Write the goals down. Writing goals forces you to clearly define your goals. It also allows you to refer to them on a daily basis. Keep your goals in the front of your mind.

4. Visualise the goals. It has been shown that people who are able to clearly visualise a goal are more likely to achieve it.[24] Here is the key though: visualise the goals as if they have already occurred. Athletes have been doing this for years and they call it mental rehearsal. "Brain studies now reveal that thoughts produce the same mental instructions as actions. Mental imagery has an impact on many cognitive processes in the brain: motor control; attention; perception; planning and memory, so that the brain is getting trained for actual performance during visualisation."[25]

   Arnold Schwarzenegger is a strong advocate for using visualisation as a method to achieve goals. Here's what he had to say about it:

   "I visualised myself being and having what it was I wanted. Before I won my first Mr. Universe title, I walked around the tournament like I owned it. I had won it so many times in my mind that there was no doubt I would win it. Then I moved on to the movies, the same thing. I visualised myself being a famous actor and earning big money. I just knew it would happen." [26]

5. Publicise your goals. By telling others about your goals, you will invoke the law of commitment and consistency upon yourself. The result is that you will feel compelled to act in a way that supports the achievement of your goal. Equally, other people may be able to help you directly or indirectly to achieve your goals.

6. Break down goals into quarterly, monthly or weekly milestones. By "chunking" a larger goal into smaller ones, it feels more achievable.

   Reaching milestones allows you to experience "wins" along the way. Little victories provide positive reinforcement of progress made to date as well as providing motivation to achieve the next milestone and the overall goal.

7. Schedule time. One of the most common reasons people fail to achieve their goals is that they don't prioritise them in their diary.

   It is critical to block time in your diary each day to focus on the most important activity that will move you to the next milestone.

   These principles are not new. I did not discover them. What I did do, however, was study successful people and the elements common to their success. These seven steps represent the synthesis of common methods used by successful people to achieve what they want from life.

   Success rarely happens by accident. To experience lasting success of any kind, you must develop the habit of setting goals.

The Importance of Habits

Success is a habit. Successful people have successful habits. Unsuccessful people have unsuccessful habits. It follows that practices that retain their patient base have habits that encourage patients to stay at the practice.

Charles Duhigg explains in his book, *The Power of Habit,* that habits are a feedback loop that consists of a trigger, an action (the habit) and a reward. With constant repetition, these habits become ingrained and action happens automatically once the trigger occurs.[27] Some habits are created intentionally but most are not.

In business, habits created intentionally are sometimes called systems. Most businesses have systems in place. The challenge is whether these systems are serving your "why" or your purpose. If they are not, old systems need to be discarded and new ones installed to replace them. Installing systems into a business takes time and conscious effort. However, once the systems are in place, the business is systemised for success.

So, when implementing the action items in this book, look at the systems in your practice. Critically analyse which ones are working and which are not. Map out the patient journey and ask yourself "How would an inspiring business do this task?" That is, remain on purpose rather than simply on task.

When implementing a new system or refining an old one, there are six steps to ensure success:

1. Pick one system at a time. You will expand on this later, but for the moment, it is important to set yourself up for an early win. Scattering your focus won't have as much impact as just choosing one thing, getting good at it and moving on to the next.

2. Come up with a plan. Analyse the existing system, look at the triggers, the action and the results. Then think of the result you'd prefer to have and decide which actions will support this. You may need to look at developing various job aids such as telephone scripts and "cheat sheets". Importantly, you will also need to identify what obstacles you will confront and plan how to overcome them.

3. Implement the system. Expect it to take four-to-six weeks before the new system begins to be ingrained.

4. Build in a positive feedback loop. A positive feedback loop will ensure positive behaviour is reinforced. Focus on your "why" and make it enjoyable and fun. You might even want to create an internal competition to keep it fun. When you have a good result, celebrate the win.

5. Report back to the team regularly. The best forum for reporting back to the team is the weekly staff meeting. Let the team know how you're progressing and continue to share and celebrate little wins as a group.

6. Test, adjust and iterate. When you implement a new system, you're testing a new approach and it is possible that it might fail and, that's normal. Knowing that your initial attempt was not successful is useful information because it's not an indication that the premise of the system is flawed. This is where many dentists say, "Yeah I tried that and it didn't work." What they're really saying is that they didn't use the information that the first attempt provided for the successive iterations – they just gave up.

Duhigg makes the point that unsuccessful people and enterprises concern themselves primarily with pleasing methods whereas successful people and enterprises are more concerned with pleasing outcomes.

Look at athletes as an example. All champion athletes have days when they don't feel like training, but what makes them champions is that they do it anyway. They have developed the habit of training, regardless of whether they feel like it or not. The sum of their habits propel them towards success. Their success also provides positive reinforcement for the continuation of those habits, creating an upward spiral of achievement.

Like athletes, successful practices have developed the habits (systems) required for success. These habits or systems, when combined with a sense of purpose, ensure the practice performs at a consistently high level and enjoys continued success.

Overcoming Obstacles

There is no doubt that as you implement the action steps in this book, you will encounter obstacles. That's normal. It's part of the journey.

As you look to implement all the strategies and tactics outlined in this book, there will inevitably come a time when you wonder if all the work is worth it. Some people may choose to quit at this point, continuing on as they have always done. Yet, somewhere in their subconscious will be a feeling of discomfort that comes from knowing they're not living to their full potential.

Why is it that some people quit while others persevere? Thomas Edison famously said that, *"Genius is 1% inspiration and 99% perspiration."* [28] – and he is right. Success of any kind takes hard work, commitment and persistence. What most lose sight of however, is the critical importance of the 1% inspiration.

The 1% inspiration that helps some push through the challenges of running their practice, comes in the form of their "why". Successful people are no more talented, lucky or blessed than any others. They persist and ultimately succeed because they are deeply connected to their purpose in life.

Your "why" should be at the front and centre of your business. By ensuring that all you do is congruent with your purpose, your "why" will come to life. Not only will your practice become a reflection of your highest ideals, your "why" will provide a guiding light to navigate any difficult times.

Paying the Price

Successful people, irrespective of their field of endeavour, have done what it takes to attain success. They have paid the price. Paying the price, or doing the work, is essential if you're going to achieve the goals and level of success that you aspire to. Vince Lombardi, the famous American Football Coach, is renowned for his quote *"there is no substitute for work."*[29]

I speak to many dentists. The most common challenge they face, at least in their minds, is a lack of patient flow. Many are looking for quick fixes to fill the appointment book now. The simple truth is that building a loyal following takes time and effort. It is going to require a vision, a commitment to excellence and hard work. The reward however, is a sustainable practice full of patients who accept treatment, pay their bills, remain loyal to the practice and refer others – a goal surely worth striving for.

As you have read through the chapters in this book, you will have seen lists of action steps. To get the most out of this book and create the practice of your dreams, you will need to complete the action items. Quite simply, do the work with a sense of purpose and specific intent and the rewards will follow.

Action Steps

1. Set goals: write them down, talk about them, visualise them and review them daily.

2. Examine your habits: are they supporting your goals? Which habits need to change? Create and implement a plan to change.

3. Anticipate obstacles and develop a contingency plan for each one.

4. Block time in your diary each day to work on your goals
   – make it a priority.

Download the Workbook

Remember to download the companion workbook to access checklists, cheat sheets and other resources. It is available at:
www.drjessegreen.com/retention/workbook

CONCLUSION

Firstly, let me thank you for taking the time to read Retention! How to Plug the #1 Profit Leak in Your Dental Practice. I hope you have enjoyed reading about some of my experiences and the lessons that I have learned along the way.

I believe that although there are challenging times ahead for the dental profession, there has never been a better time to build a remarkable practice and a loyal following. To do that, however, means adapting to the new reality. What worked in the past doesn't work now and won't in the future. To survive, dentists will need to think and act differently.

We only get one crack at life and our work is such a large part of it that I believe we should accept nothing less than our best efforts as we go about our craft. Ultimately, being remarkable is not just about building an awesome practice, it is about doing our best work and deriving a sense of fulfilment that comes from that.

Our patients are people, just like us, who have the same hopes, fears and aspirations as we do. To be remarkable and build a loyal following, it is essential to be a student of the human condition – what motivates us, what upsets us, and what's important to us.

I have outlined the key components I have used to attract and retain patients in my own practices. What I have explained may seem simple to you, however, I can assure you that building a loyal following takes effort, commitment and persistence.

It is my fervent wish that as you have read this book, you have made a list of the key lessons you're going to apply to your own practice on a daily basis. Commit to a timetable and make it happen – nothing changes if nothing changes.

I truly hope that I have inspired to you realise that if you build a remarkable practice, you'll never have to worry about patient flow again.

ACKNOWLEDGEMENTS

Writing a book is a team effort and I have been very fortunate to have worked with some truly outstanding people over the past eighteen months.

Firstly I'd like to thank my patients past and present. You have each taught me valuable lessons and helped to improve our practice one increment at a time.

To Andrew Griffiths, Australia's leading small business author, I thank you for your guidance, direction, feedback and support. You have shown incredible generosity of spirit and I am truly grateful.

To my editor Tamara Protassow, without you this book would never have been completed. Thank you for believing in me and what I have to say. Your good nature and naughty sense of humour have kept me sane throughout the process of writing this book.

To my best mate David Dugan, thank you for your support and care. You're *always* there and I appreciate that so very much.

Lastly, I would like to acknowledge the endless love and support I receive from my family. Miranda, Jemima and Maisie – you are my "why". I love the three of you more than you can imagine.

ABOUT DR JESSE GREEN

Dr Jesse Green is a dentist and entrepreneur with a passion for helping dentists create a business and a life that they love. He is a best-selling author, dynamic presenter and accredited performance coach.

Jesse's passion for business began at a young age. His first business venture involved selling branded football jerseys to his peers at high school. It was this first taste of commerce that lit his entrepreneurial flame that still burns brightly today.

After university, Jesse spent several years as a dentist in the Navy. During this time, he came to understand the vital role of leadership in success and the value of strong operating processes.

When he entered private practice he was able to apply this experience to his businesses with great success. He has purchased, turned around and sold several dental practices in both the pre and post-GFC economies.

Inspired to help others reach their full potential, Jesse created Practice Max, a high performance business mastermind. Practice Max is far more than a training program; it is a community of dentists, each striving for the highest levels of success, united by the belief that there has never been a better time to build a practice.

Jesse is an avid traveller and a cricket tragic. Sadly, his own cricketing career was cut short due to an acute lack of talent. These days he is content to travel and watch from the stands.

Jesse lives in Canberra and is married with two daughters.

SPEAKING OPPORTUNITIES

Dr Jesse Green is a sought after speaker whose key message is that "there has never been a better time to own a dental practice".

His presentations are highly engaging, motivational and intensely practical, equipping people to get results in the real world.

Jesse uses a series of tools, anecdotes and how-to's combined with a self deprecating sense of humour and laid back style to take his audience on a journey to unlock their practice's potential.

Some of Jesse's favourite topics to speak on are:

1. Making competition irrelevant
2. How to win more patients
3. How to build and lead great teams
4. Building a "Scaled" practice
5. Maximising the personal performance of the business leader

For more information, bookings and bulk book sales:

Email: hello@drjessegreen.com
Phone: 1300 66 83 84 (Australia)

PRACTICE MAX PROGRAM

The Practice Max Program is a high performance business mastermind that takes dental practice owners to a level of performance far beyond what is achievable with traditional practice management methods.

The program is designed for those dentists looking to maximise the performance of their dental practice or looking to scale their operations. It has a strong emphasis on implementation and personal performance, while covering seven core strengths that help dentists have more patients, more profits and less stress.

1. Values
2. Leadership
3. Financial Intelligence
4. Smart Systems
5. Case Acceptance
6. Art of Marketing
7. Winning team

Our tailored program is delivered via 1:1 business coaching, quarterly workshops and monthly webinars as well as access to a resource vault containing tools, templates, systems and strategies.

More than just a training program, Practice Max is a community that appeals to dentists who are entrepreneurially minded and committed to the highest level of professional success.

Over 18 months our clients typically increase their revenue by 47% while working less. Participants consistently give feedback that the results they achieve on the program far exceed what they could have accomplished on their own.

For more information on the Practice Max Program visit:
drjessegreen.com/practice-max or email hello@drjessegreen.com

SOCIAL MEDIA

To receive the latest insights, updates and resources, follow Jesse on social media:

Websites: drjessegreen.com
Facebook: facebook.com/drjessegreen
LinkedIn: au.linkedin.com/in/drjessegreen
Twitter: twitter.com/drjessegreen

ENDNOTES

Chapter 1

1. Health Workforce Australia 2013, Health workforce by numbers, HWA, Canberra, viewed 11 Jan 14
   http://www.hwa.gov.au/sites/uploads/HWA_Health-Workforce-by-Numbers_Issue-2_LR.pdf

2. Middleton, G 2013, 'The dental numbers disaster' Australasian Dental Practice April - May, pp84-88. viewed 26 June 2013
   http://www.synstrat.com.au/PDFs/dentistarticlesThe%2Dental%2Numbers%20Disaster%20of%202013%20April.pdf

3. Dental Board of Australia 2013, Consultation paper-Draft Scope of practice registration standard and guidelines, AHPRA, Canberra. Viewed 18 May 2013
   http://www.dentalboard.gov.au

4. Insight Economics 2013, Demand for dental services in Australia, ADA, Sydney. page 32 viewed 11 Jan 14
   http://www.ada.org.au/app_cmslib/media/lib/1309/m682920_v1_dental_demand_in_australia.pdf

5. Parnell, S 2013, 'NIB Health fund to offer medical tourism' The Australian viewed online 11 January 2014
   http://www.theaustralian.com.au/news/health-science/nib-health-fund-to-offer-medical-tourism/story-e6frg8y6-1226747206131#

6. Adriani, F, Deidda, L 2006 Competition and the signalling role of prices viewed 11 November 2013
   http://www.cefims.ac.uk/documents/research-52.pdf

Chapter 3

7. Sinek, S 2011, Start with why : how great leaders inspire everyone to take action, Penguin Putnam Inc, New York.

8. Hsieh T, Delivering Happiness : a path to profits, passion and purpose, Little Brown and Company, New York

Chapter 4

9. Pease, A 2008, Questions are the answers, Manjul Publishing House, Bhopal.

10. Covey, SR 1999, The 7 habits of highly effective people ; powerful lessons in personal change, Simon and Schuster, London.

11. Covey, SMR 2006, The speed of trust: the one thing that changes everything, Free Press, New York.

12. Blanchard, K, Olmstead, C, & Lawrence M, 2013, Trust works: four keys to building lasting relationships, Harper Collins Publishers, London.

13. John Maxwell quotes, viewed 13 September 2013 http://www.goodreads.com/quotes/34690-people-don-t-care-how-much-you-know-until-they-know

14. Brown, B 2013, Daring greatly: how the courage to be vulnerable transforms the way we live, love, parent, and lead, Penguin Putnam Inc, New York.

15. Conkle, A 2008 'Serious research on happiness' Observer Association for Psychological Science, vol. 21 no. 7 viewed 23 October 2014 http://www.psychologicalscience.org/index.php/video/serious-research-on-happiness.html

Chapter 5

16. Gitomer, J 1998, Customer satisfaction is worthless, customer loyalty is priceless : how to make them love you, keep them coming back, and tell everyone they know, Bard Press, Austin

17. Michel, S, Bowen, D, Johnston R, 2008 'Making the most of customer complaints' Wall Street Journal Online 22 September, viewed 22 November 2013. http://online.wsj.com/news/articles/SB122160026028144779

Chapter 6

18. Cialdini, R 2007, Influence : the psychology of persuasion, Harper Collins Publishers Inc, New York.

Chapter 8

19. Gladwell, M 2001, The Tipping Point: How Little Things Can Make a Big Difference, Little Brown Book Group, London.

20. Kennedy, D 2011, The ultimate marketing plan: Target your audience! Get out your message! Build your brand, Adams Media Corporation, Holbrook, MA.

Chapter 9

21. Gallo, C 2012, The apple experience: secrets to building insanely great customer loyalty, McGraw-Hill Education, New York.

22. Colllins, J 2004, Good to great, Cornerstone, London

Chapter 10

23. McCormack, M 1994, What they don't teach you at Harvard Business School, Profile Business, London.

24. Grohol, JM 2011, 'Visualise your goal in order to attain it' Psych Central, 16 August, viewed 27 June 2014
http://psychcentral.com/news/2011/08/16/visualize-your-goal-in-order-to-attain-it/28624.html

25. LeVan, A 2009, 'Seeing is Believing: The Power of Visualisation', Psychology Today, 3 December, viewed 23 January 2014
http://www.psychologytoday.com/blog/flourish/200912/seeing-is-believing-the-power-visualization

26. Arnold Schwarzenegger quotes, viewed 1 April 2014
http://m.imdb.com/name/nm0000216/quotes

27. Duhigg, C 2012, The power of habit: why we do what we do, and how to change, Cornerstone, London.

28. Thomas Edison quotes, viewed 1 April 2014
http://www.brainyquote.com/quotes/authors/t/thomas_a_edison_2.html

29. Vince Lombardi quotes, viewed 17 May 2014
http://www0.nfl.packers.com/team/coaches/lombardi_vince/quotes/

30. Five key ways to build customer relationships 2005, Entrepreneur Magazine, viewed online 1 January 14
http://www.entrepreneur.com/article/77686

www.ingramcontent.com/pod-product-compliance
Lightning Source LLC
Chambersburg PA
CBHW030523210326
41597CB00013B/1007